PRAISE FOR
Jay Ciniglio's ulti

Shape magazine . . .
"*JayWalking* is the most clever outdoor walking expedition."

Self magazine . . .
"When it comes to working out, the outdoors is in . . . Take a morning fitness walk and *JayWalk* your way into a whole new day."

Fitness magazine . . .
"Try *JayWalking* and go on a mental tour of various parks, gardens, and hiking trails . . . This is it."

Exercise for Men magazine . . .
"You'll truly change your perception of what walking is. *JayWalking* is motivational and creates a mind-set of tranquillity and stress-reduction."

New Woman magazine . . .
"What an awesome class!!!"

Dr. Stephan Rechtschaffen, M.D., and author of *Timeshifting,* **President of the Omega Institute for Holistic Studies . . .**
"*JayWalking: The Ultimate Fitness Journey* is an energizing approach to fostering ultimate health of body, mind, and spirit. It is a holistic journey focusing on each individual's ability to improve quality of life by using a variety of techniques, enhancing the simple act of walking. *JayWalking* is inspiring, enthusiastic, and empowering."

Susan Jeffers, Ph.D., author of *Feel the Fear and Do It Anyway* **. . .**
"With his charismatic charm and wisdom, Jay really knows how to motivate his readers to walk the walk. Not only will you lace up your walking shoes, but you'll feel the fear and do it anyway!"

Rosanna Scotto (anchor, *Fox 5 News,* **N.Y., N.Y.) . . .**
"After my second pregnancy, and an additional sixty pounds, Jay and the *JayWalking* fitness program has helped me to melt away the fat and inches and brought me back to my ideal weight. Way to go, Jay!"

Robin Strasser (Emmy Award–winning actress of ABC's *One Life to Live) . . .*
"A journey begins with the first step. *JayWalking* has everything you need to know about one of the most user-friendly ways to keep fit—walking, and it's fun!"

JAYWALKING®

The Ultimate Fitness Journey

JAY CINIGLIO

photos by

ROBERT VANCE BLOSSER

BERKLEY BOOKS, NEW YORK

This book is an original publication of The Berkley Publishing Group.
JayWalking is a registered trademark belonging to Jay Ciniglio.

JAYWALKING

A Berkley Book / published by arrangement with
the author

PRINTING HISTORY
Berkley trade paperback edition / September 1998

The Penguin Putnam Inc. World Wide Web site address is http://www.penguinputnam.com

ISBN: 0-425-16310-5

BERKLEY®
Berkley Books are published by The Berkley Publishing Group,
a member of Penguin Putnam Inc.,
200 Madison Avenue, New York, New York 10016.
BERKLEY and the "B" design
are trademarks belonging to Berkley Publishing Corporation.

PRINTED IN THE UNITED STATES OF AMERICA

10 9 8 7 6 5 4 3 2 1

C O N T E N T S

The words, thoughts, and feelings I express in this book began with the foundation of my upbringing. My family life and childhood were a far cry from Disneyland. However, with all of the dysfunction I did encounter as a child, there was one thing my immediate family always instilled, and that was unconditional love. I consider myself one of the fortunate ones. You've all been there for me. I love you with all of my heart. This book is dedicated to you, Grandma, Grandpa, Mom, Dad, and Peter. God bless.

ACKNOWLEDGMENTS

Even though my name appears as the author of this book, behind every successful man are many other fabulous men and women. Without them, where would I be? My sincere thanks go out to:

New York Sports Club for the continued support of the JayWalking program;

exercise physiologists Geralyn Cooper-Smith, M.A., Ann Marie Miller, M.A., Michael Youssauf, M.A., and nutritionist Abby Greenspun, M.S., R.D., CDN;

my spectacular editor and friend Jessica Faust, who made me look good—thanks, Jess;

my amazing literary agent, Dominick Abel—you have been a storehouse of knowledge;

my photographer, Robert Vance Blosser;

my makeup artist, Laura Geller and the Laura Geller Studios;

my logo designers, Jill Korostoff and crew of JAK Design;

my hairstylist, Avi Mizrahi;

my fashion consultants, Susan Hoxie, Virginia Sullivan, and Sharon Rapsiek;

my lawyers, Michael G. Marinangeli, Esq., and Richard Stoll;

my supporters and teachers, Marilyn Coccoza Trillo, Herci Marsden, Laurie Brager, Katherine Gertz, Jan Aaron, Christine Kerrigan, Jeffrey Vincent Noble, Susan Jeffers for her guidance and professional support and Rachel Sibony;

Unity Center of New York, for the spiritual guidance, and associate minister Paul Tenaglia for his time and inspiring words;

and a special and humbling thanks to my good friend Thomas Boyce, whose literary skills and motivational support were there when I needed them most; without you this book could have never been done—thank you, Tom, from the bottom of my heart;

and last, but not least, thanks to all of you JayWalkers out there, present and future, who participate in the JayWalking fitness philosophy. It is your consistent efforts that make JayWalking the Ultimate Fitness Journey!

INTRODUCTION

Imagine being able to create a lean, sculpted body in moments a day! Imagine having a higher level of self-esteem and motivation to achieve all of your unfulfilled dreams! Imagine that you can experience a sound body, mind, and spirit, and escape the pressures of life, without a structured fitness program!

Well, gang, it's finally here, and it's *JayWalking*. No, no, no, not the pedestrian violation, but a walking program designed for you to achieve fitness, well-being, and a higher quality of life.

Most of you probably think of exercising as a tedious process. I'm here to tell you otherwise. While reading and practicing JayWalking, you will discover that fitness is not about sweating in a health club. It is not about what you see in the mirror. It is about what can be revealed to you in each and every moment of your life. It is about who you are, not what you are.

Walking takes no special skill—in fact, it's probably something you do every day. But that doesn't mean it can't be a monumental experience. What happened the first time your parents let go of your hands, allowing you to take those first few baby steps? Suddenly you were free to move on your own. And for that you were rewarded with love, encouragement, and confidence. So why shouldn't you feel good about walking now? My theory is, no matter how much we take walking for granted, it is something we should all be proud of.

It's amazing to me how we as a society don't trust ourselves. We are so busy looking outside of ourselves that we dismiss our own unique and hidden talents. I was blessed at a young age to meet first-grade dance teacher Miss Doris. She taught me how to trust my instincts. Every year she led her tiny prodigies in a dance recital. That was the time when all of our blood, sweat, and tears paid off. We were finally in the spotlight. I'll never forget the fear of a seven-year-old. I was terrified of not being able to remember all my dance steps. With a calming smile Miss Doris turned to me and said, "Jay, just keep your chin up, put on a happy grin, and never look down at your feet. For even if you make a mistake no one will ever notice as long as you're smiling wide."

Looking back now I realize that her philosophy was not just meant for a seven-year-old at a dance recital. It is a belief I have carried with me throughout my life and straight into JayWalking. JayWalking has no set rules or restrictions. If you forget one or two techniques, you can make something up: clap your hands, sing a song, chant a word, or just keep your arms swinging.

The bottom line is, if you make a commitment to do anything in life, even if it seems uncomfortable and not believable at first, fake it till you make it, go through the motions and keep smiling. There's no way you can fail as long as you show up, and with JayWalking you can't ever fail. Be aware of what is revealed to you and in the process your unique answers will be shown to you. There is no wrong; everything is right. So join me now in discovering why *JayWalking is the ultimate fitness journey.*

WHAT IS JAYWALKING?

The 1980s are considered to be the dawn of the fitness revolution. Health clubs began dotting the American landscape and psyche. The body became the center of our attention and celebrities endorsed countless fitness programs, machines, and diets. The "no pain, no gain" generation was in full swing.

The belief was that the more the exercise hurt and the more time we put in, the quicker we'd see results and the healthier we'd become. High-impact. High-stress. High-fiber. High-anxiety.

Like every other fitness fanatic, I decided to keep up with the times and obsess over carbohydrates and starch, vitamin supplements and fad diets. I looked upon relaxation and calmness and fatty foods with equal and utter contempt. My frustration and unhappiness mounted when my body never measured up to that sleek, sculpted look the media had imposed and that I had so badly wanted.

Fueled by feelings of self-defeat and hopelessness, I'd run back to the health club for two hours of high-intensity exercise. Before I realized it, it was 11 P.M., the gym was closing for the night, and I was in no better shape then when I walked in the door. On top of it all, I *hated* every moment of that exercise routine. What really frustrates me now is that most people still think this relentless approach is the only way to achieve fitness.

So what exactly is it that makes individuals beat themselves up, day after day, night after night? One day it finally dawned on me: *lack!* We're so busy focusing on what we don't have, what we think we need, that we never find happiness with what we do have, with our good points. I finally realized that if I were to continue on with this belief and mentality, I would never reap the physical fitness benefits I was struggling toward.

The beauty of JayWalking is that you will come from a place of abundance, focusing on all of your unexpressed talents and gifts. You will learn to enjoy quiet time. You will begin to appreciate how wonderful it is to live on this earth, to stand on your own two feet, to be present. Not only will your physical being improve, but so will your mind. JayWalking is about optimum health.

Optimum health means having balance—a balance of healthy thoughts that make you feel good about yourself, the world, and the people around you. According to Chinese Taoism, everything in the universe, including us, is composed of various proportions of the yin and yang polarities. Yin is receptive (open to other perceptions without judgment—just being). Yang is the energy of doing (walking, thinking, moving). When these energies work in synch, our actions have purpose and meaning. We begin to feel energized and fulfilled. And when they don't, we feel drained and frustrated. This is what JayWalking is all about: the balance of these energies and your ability to keep them that way.

JayWalking: The Ultimate Fitness Journey is not just another approach to fitness, but a whole new approach to well-being. JayWalking takes the time to focus on your mind and spirit, not just your body. In other words, it isn't just about *doing* something, but about *being* something.

Unlike any other fitness program, JayWalking incorporates three levels of consciousness, or three journeys, each just as important as the other. JayWalking is not meant to be a fad. It is meant to be a lifestyle.

In order to be truly healthy, you must look at the total you. This means looking at the conscious mind, the subconscious mind, and the superconscious. The decision to separate JayWalking into three journeys comes from my belief that people's challenges are from one of three areas: thought (mental), body (physical), or emotions (spiritual).

The conscious mind is the state in which we are actively aware of our thoughts. It is also the site of our *Mental Journey*, the beginning of the JayWalking program. The mental journey allows us to create energy, optimism, and joy, to break through procrastination, and get on with the tasks at hand. This journey can be applied to any area of your life, to make you feel powerful and in control.

This subconscious mind is the storehouse of our memories, where our past thoughts and feelings lie. It is in the *Physical Journey* that you truly build a relationship with your body. Here you learn how to create a fun and versatile fitness program all your own, instead of following a rigid calendar. Here is where you begin to change all that you've been taught about fitness. This is probably why you bought the book and will be the easiest journey for you to follow. After all, whenever you have an opportunity to walk, you can opt to JayWalk.

The final part of our journey is the superconscious mind, or the *Spiritual Journey*. This is the part of us that receives inspiration, ideas, creativity, and love. This is our natural intellect. The spiritual journey is the journey of perfect ideas. It explores those parts of our life we are most concerned with: our relationships, career, aging— anything that makes us who we are. The spiritual journey cannot be achieved until the mental and physical journeys are applied.

JayWalking is not just for the fitness enthusiast, but for anyone who believes that he or she has the power to improve his or her life. JayWalking can be done alone or in a group, anytime and anywhere. JayWalking can be done in a suit at the office, while mowing the lawn, or at the beach. It isn't just about getting in shape, but about taking responsibility for our actions and lifting our awareness to the highest state we can achieve.

As it has done for me, my JayWalking program will self-motivate you, and the more motivated you are, the greater the possibilities are for fulfilling your true potential in life. This book is dedicated to the philosophy that fitness is found within. Enjoy your journey.

JAYWALKING®

*The Ultimate
Fitness Journey*

GETTING STARTED

Whatever you can do, or
dream you can, begin it.

Boldness has genius, power,
and magic in it.

—GOETHE

DRESS FOR SUCCESS

SHOES

As with any exercise program, you need to start out with the proper equipment, and that usually includes the proper footwear. The beauty of JayWalking is that it is a state of mind, as well as a philosophy, and can be done anytime and anywhere, in any footwear. You can JayWalk barefoot on the beach, in high heels down a crowded avenue, or in boots in the middle of a January blizzard. However, to get the physical fitness benefits of an optimum workout, I recommend—you guessed it—a comfortable pair of walking sneakers. Good sneakers will be worth their weight in gold in the long . . . walk!

Buying a good sneaker doesn't just mean walking into any store and grabbing the cheapest thing on the shelf. There are a number of things to look for when shopping for your new JayWalking shoes. In addition, I would recommend that you try on sneakers late in the day, as opposed to early in the morning. This way your feet are slightly swelled, and you'll get a better fit.

Weight: You don't want a heavy sneaker. Even hikers prefer a lightweight boot. This saves wear and tear on your joints. Keep an eye out for shoes specially made for walking or running. These are often lighter than other kinds of sneakers.

Comfort: If your feet aren't happy, you won't be happy. I can't stress this enough. Take time to try on many different brands.

Size: Can you wiggle your toes a little? Good! There should be a thumb's width between your big toe and the front of your sneaker. This will give room for your foot to expand. Keep in mind new shoes are a lot like new jeans; they need to be broken in. If you're not sure of the fit, take them home and walk around a carpeted area for a while. If it doesn't seem like your new shoes are any more comfortable, you should exchange them for a new pair.

Support: Does your foot feel secure? Is it cushioned on the bottom and braced on the sides? Cushioning and arch support should be just right. Your heels should not be lifting too high out of the shoe, as this can cause blistering. A good walking sneaker should move with your foot naturally.

Flexibility: Your sneakers should bend where your foot bends, from the moment you put them on. Be especially aware of the spot directly underneath the base of the toes. You want the shoe to keep your foot stable, but you also want it to allow your foot to move in its natural motion. To test out your sneaker for flexibility, hold the shoe by the heel and toe. Flex it up from the toe; it should bend where the ball of your foot would be.

Mid-Sole: The point directly below your arch should be slightly firm, to increase the durability of your shoe.

Cut: I don't recommend high-tops for JayWalking. High-top sneakers tend to restrict movement. Sneakers used for walking or running should be low-tops, exposing your ankle. Keep those ankles free in order to flex them as you work out.

Materials: You don't want your feet to sweat up a storm, do you? Dry feet are happy feet (unless you're fond of athlete's foot). New lightweight materials and lots of ventilation holes will help keep your feet dry.

Socks: I never thought socks were as important as they are until I began walking marathons. If you're prone to blistering, try to find a slip-sock that has two layers sewed into one. The outside layer is cotton, the inside layer is nylon, wicking moisture away and allow-

> ### WHERE SHOULD I BUY MY WALKING SHOES?
>
> I recommend any good sports shoe store. They will have a variety of prices and styles. As long as you're comfortable and happy with your shoe, stick with the same model and company. It isn't a bad idea to buy a second pair of shoes and wear them on alternate days; this way your shoes will last longer.
>
> *How often should I buy a new pair of sneakers?*
> As a general rule, walking shoes tend to wear out after about four hundred miles. This would be every four months, if you walk four or five days a week.
>
> *When do I know my walking shoes are worn out?*
> All walkers are different. Some are light walkers, some are heavy. Walking shoes can wear out in many areas. Waiting until there are holes in the soles and your feet begin to ache would be pushing yourself, and your shoes, to the limit. Rule of thumb: Pay attention to the areas outside the bottom of the heel and under your big toe. If the sole becomes thin and fragile in these areas, it's time to go shopping.

ing your foot to slide against the outer cotton layer. If you have small feet, check with specific manufacturers for specialty sizes. Too much sock will create bulking in the toe-box.

APPAREL

It was proven to me one hot day in early January that what you wear on your body is just as important as what you wear on your feet. Your attire can make or break a good workout. I learned the hard way that it isn't just what you wear, but when you wear it. January in New York isn't typically warm, and especially not hot, so I prepared myself for a frigid winter day. Bundled up, I headed to the park in a T-shirt, two sweatshirts, a scarf, earmuffs, gloves, and jacket. Warmly dressed and comfortable, I felt very confident and well prepared for an energizing JayWalk. However, as my walk progressed and my body began to heat up, I sensed that I was in trouble. With so many clothes on, my body began to overheat and I started to feel like I couldn't breathe. Removing layer after layer in

an attempt to cool down, it wasn't long before I turned into a walking clothes rack.

When preparing for your JayWalk, it is important not only to
know the weather conditions, but also to be aware of how your body
reacts to temperature. Are you a hot or cold person? By having the
proper guidelines, you can quickly get dressed for an invigorating
walk in any kind of weather.

Warm Weather

I find that hot weather apparel lends itself to lightweight cottons
and/or nylon blend fabrics that are loosely fitting to permit air circulation.

In the summer months I prefer to wear shorts, T-shirts, and lightweight socks. It is also a good idea to wear a baseball cap and/or sun-
glasses to protect your head and eyes from the sun. And, of course,
you can't forget the sunscreen and insect repellent. I have found that
sport sunscreens with an SPF of 15 to 30 work best. These are wonderful products that are light, non-greasy, non-irritating, and hypoal-
lergenic. Some even come with built-in insect repellent.

Cold Weather

Of course, cold weather takes a bit more planning and prepara-
tion. However, a blizzard has never stopped me from JayWalking—or
most of my clients. In fact, exercising outdoors during the winter
months can be a whole new experience. Crisp air, snow-covered
landscapes, and brooks candied with ice can be just the solution to
a stressful day. Think of how tranquil and serene the sights and
sounds of winter can be. Cooler temperatures shouldn't be an excuse
to lock yourself in a confining health club, or quit working out alto-
gether. Just remember, the key to winter workouts is *layering*.

Your first layer should consist of a lightweight synthetic fabric
such as nylon or polypropylene. This will help pull perspiration away
from the body, keeping you dryer and warmer. This layer should be
fitted to your body to keep cold air out. Try thermal, insulated, or silk
tights, which fit closely to the legs.

Your second layer should consist of a sweatshirt made of cotton,
fleece, wool, or one of the newer synthetic piles like Polartec. These

fabrics will absorb moisture, keep the warmth in, and let your skin breathe. Sweatpants or nylon- or cotton-lined running trousers should be worn on your legs.

Finally, cover it all up with a water-resistant or waterproof jacket, such as a windbreaker, anorak, or parka made of a lightweight nylon blend.

When dressing for winter walking many people forget about their extremities. Keeping your head, hands, and neck warm will help keep the rest of you warm. Don't forget your hat, scarf, and mittens. Yes, mittens! Mittens will keep your hands warmer than gloves because they allow your body heat to stay more contained.

Even in winter you need a sports moisturizer and sunscreen to protect your skin from chafing and sunburn. It is also a good idea to wear a good lip balm. Don't scoff at that winter sun!

COLOR FOR SUCCESS

Dressing for JayWalking doesn't have to be just about comfort; it is also about looking and feeling good. I have discovered that one of the most immediate emotional changes comes from color. By wearing certain colors you can change your perception of who and what you are. Color can help increase our self-esteem and energy level, or bring us to a place of tranquility and confidence.

When choosing colors to wear, you may want to ask yourself, *What do I want to feel today?* or *What do I want to portray?* (Examples: enthusiasm, life, energy, humor, intelligence, warmth, graciousness.) Think for a moment about how the colors of nature have such a subtle influence on our daily life. The bright pinks of an early morning sunrise or the multicolored flowers of a spring day each create underlying emotional changes. Color, like a box of crayons with a coloring book, brings the black-and-white pages to life.

When putting together your JayWalking outfit, take note of the colors to see how they influence your emotional state and mood. Notice what colors you favor and why, and think about experimenting. Have some fun!

Red: Great when you need a little get up and go. This color creates confidence, happiness, and an adventurous attitude. Excellent when you want to be noticed. Avoid wearing red when extremely overstressed or confrontational, as this can aggravate your anxiety.

Blue: Like a clear blissful sky, or the warm tropical ocean, the color blue symbolizes peace, tranquility, consistency, and healing. Blue is not uplifting and may not be the best color choice if you are lacking energy.

Yellow: Yellow and yellow tones are attributed to optimism, cheer, warmth, and action. A great JayWalking color. Avoid yellow when you're angry or confused. It may delay your internal process of finding your underlying turmoil.

Green: I was once told by a spiritual advisor that to bring prosperity into my life I should burn green candles. Well, I did, and guess what—it worked! Green is powerful, rejuvenating, dependable, and comforting. Wearing green will humble you and make you worthy of exceptional things. Green is especially lucky on St. Patrick's Day, when you've got the luck of the Irish.

Pink: One of my favorite colors—I've always loved the vividness of bright pinks. Pink tones exude gentleness and an inviting demeanor. An excellent color if you want to meet new people; it makes you very accessible. Avoid wearing pink in situations where you want to keep to yourself.

Purple, Violet and Lilac: Passion. The color of intrigue and royalty. Wearing purple can help you develop an artistic imagination, a higher level of intuition, and a keen sensitivity. Avoid purple if you are trying to keep a low profile and want to be left alone.

Orange: Active, alive, enthusiastic, gregarious. Orange is a very fun color. Great for JayWalking at dusk, for you won't be missed. Avoid orange if you are out to impress a prospective mate, as it has the tendency to come off too strong. It is also not a good color to choose when you are dieting, for you may get overzealous and splurge.

White: Once you've completed all three JayWalking journeys, you will never wear white the same way again. White produces clarity, cleansing, spirituality, and freshness, all of which are an integral part of my fitness philosophy. White is a great reflector of the sun's rays and a wonderful complement to any other color in the spectrum.

Use this color to achieve inner peace. Avoid dingy yellowed whites, for they will hinder you from walking with clarity and awareness.

Brown: Autumn brings forth the earthy tones of nature. It is the ideal time for harvesting. Wearing the neutral colors of brown creates a homey, inviting, comforting quality. If you are not prepared to play therapist or mom for the day, avoid wearing brown.

Black: The only color which contains all colors of the spectrum. Black promotes sophistication, mystery, and strength. An excellent color to add to your bold, vivid tones. Avoid wearing all black if you want to be open and receptive to people around you.

Happy trails and a successful walk can all depend on safety. Without proper awareness of our body, our surroundings, and the hazards that are possible on our journey, we open ourselves up to many uninvited guests. To decrease the likelihood of any unpleasant experience, the rule of thumb for a safe walk is to be confident and use common sense.

In any self-defense seminar you might attend, the number one rule is to appear strong and to walk with confidence. As you will learn in the *Physical Journey,* the JayWalking technique is structured to exude strength, security, and confidence, which will greatly decrease your chances of ever attracting negative energy.

Make a special note to be conscious of the color of your clothing (see pages 7–9). If you plan on walking in the evening hours, it is best to wear light or even reflective clothing.

WARM WEATHER SAFETY

As I mentioned in the section on clothing, it is very important to be aware of the weather conditions. In hot weather there is only one word to remember: water, water, and more water. Before any hot weather outdoor activity, be sure to properly hydrate. I have learned from experience that during the hottest months of the summer one should avoid outdoor JayWalking between the hours of 11 A.M. and 5 P.M. This is when the sun is at its height, and air pollution is on the rise. Of course you can always take this time to visit a local shopping mall. Remember this is never a bad place to JayWalk, and a little shopping couldn't hurt anyone.

Without enough water, hyperthermia—or heat stroke—can be a danger to JayWalkers. Hyperthermia is a common condition that can happen to anyone who works too hard in the heat. Dizziness, light-headedness, rapid pulse, and nausea are all symptoms. Remember, the human body cannot work as rapidly in hot weather, and it may take several weeks to adjust to the heat. Relax, and calmly ask your-self, *Where's the fire?* Enjoy the warm weather, seasonal foliage, fragrant aromas, and the sun's rays. You may have to slow yourself down in hot weather—so what. Don't judge. Gradually you will be able to get back up to your normal pace.

Keep in mind that the body cannot absorb more than one liter of water per hour, even in hot weather. My recommendation would be to drink at least eight to ten ounces of water before your work out, and another eight to ten midway through.

COLD WEATHER SAFETY

Guess what? Drinking water before you JayWalk is just as important in cold weather as it is in hot weather. In cooler temperatures your perspiration will evaporate more quickly, giving you the sense that you are not perspiring as readily. Don't be fooled. Even in cool weather your body can become dehydrated, and it is important to always drink a lot of water.

However, my greatest concern with my classes during the cold months is not how much water everyone is drinking, but black ice. I'm sure you've seen it: those fine, thin patches of ice that develop on the pavement and look like an oil slick. This is why I recommend always keeping your head up and looking straight ahead, as though you are driving a car. Remember, the key to black ice is knowing what to do. When walking across an icy patch, it is important to keep your feet separated, bend your knees, relax, and by all means slow down. You can always increase your pace later. Play it safe.

FIRST AID

Safety when JayWalking also means careful first aid. Although JayWalking is virtually injury-free, sprains and strains can occur during a walk. Just remember, the best way to recover from an injury is to get lots of rest.

The key to a safe and successful JayWalk is stretching. Stretching is not only important before and after your JayWalk, but also anytime you have an injury. If you are injured, it is important to nurture, embrace, and pamper the tender area. Static stretching, which is a stretch that you continuously hold for fifteen to thirty seconds, is tremendously helpful in alleviating sore tendons and ligaments. I also recommend aspirin or a non-aspirin pain reliever to help reduce swelling and curb the unpleasant aches, pains, and soreness.

One of the most common injuries with walking, or taking part in any other sport, is a sprain. The most important thing to have on hand for a sprain is RICE. And I don't mean the San Francisco treat.

Rest, Ice, Compression, Elevation.

Rest: Resting is extremely important to allow damaged or inflamed tissue to repair without further injury. This means staying off your feet as much as possible, or avoiding any activity that exasperates the injured area.

Ice: Ice is a miracle cure for many sprains. It will immediately reduce swelling and promote healing. Ice or ice packs should be applied at fifteen minute intervals, removed for five minutes, and repeated frequently for the first forty-eight hours. Generally after forty-eight hours you can switch to heat or alternate ice and heat. For serious injuries consult your physician.

Compression: Placing pressure, either with your hands or with an elastic wrap, aids in the reduction of swelling. This pressure will help force the fluids from the injured area back into the drainage system.

Elevation: By elevating the injured area, you allow gravity to move fluids away from the injury and back into the drainage system. When elevating a sprain, it is important to keep the injured area above heart level.

Many people, especially beginning JayWalkers, can develop cramping during their walk. This is a common problem, especially in the early spring or the late fall, when the seasons are changing, or when you travel to a different climate. When your body is subjected to changes in temperature, the levels of electrolytes—potassium, magnesium, and sodium, to name a few—become imbalanced. The results are those familiar, uncomfortable, sharp stabbing pains. If you feel any cramping when JayWalking, slow down, breathe, and visually focus on releasing its hold on you, for it too shall pass.

THE MENTAL JOURNEY

*A mind once expanded can
never contract to its
original size.*

—RALPH WALDO EMERSON

INTRODUCTION

I think it would be fair to say that in order to take any action in life, we must first have a concept, a thought, or an idea. Therefore, as part of my complete fitness program, the Mental Journey must precede all other journeys. It is the spark that creates the continually burning flame. Without a proper mental attitude, one cannot expect to achieve the optimum fitness effects of JayWalking.

In The Mental Journey, you will discover the dynamic tools I have amassed that have kept me motivated and consistent in Jay-Walking and all other aspects of my life. Think of how exciting it can be to discover exercises and techniques that will help you become a more motivated, humble, sincere, loving, and caring person. As with any other experience in life, one should take what one needs and throw the rest away. My suggestion is to handle the information as you would change in your pocket; when you need it, it's there to bail you out.

I firmly believe we are exactly where we need to be at any given moment in our lives. Everything is perfect just the way it is. But what does that mean? How can everything be perfect if I lost my job, I have no money, or I hate my body? That is what the mental journey is all about. Each of our discomforts and struggles in life happen for a reason, and in the Mental Journey you will discover how and why getting through it all only makes you stronger.

The most important thing to remember when embarking on your Mental Journey is that the harder the struggle, the more enjoyable the reward. In order to achieve permanent change in our lives, we must first begin to look at our emotional discomforts and pains. This is the most challenging and courageous act humans can undertake. We love to candy-coat our lives, place blame on others, run to alcohol, food, and drugs, and focus on our physical faults. Anything to avoid looking at our emotional discomforts. It is human nature to do anything in our power to avoid pain and create pleasure.

I remember waking up one morning to a gray and dreary sky and finding it was easier to stay in bed than to commit to my JayWalking routine. I felt like a schoolchild playing hooky for the day. Mom and Dad weren't home, so I'd pull the covers over my head, sink into a soft, billowy pillow, and fall back into a safe, restful slumber. A few hours later, I'd awaken with a coy grin on my face, thinking I had gotten away with something.

So why is it, if I had done exactly what I wanted, done something that supposedly made me happy, that I felt so miserable? Instead of making an attempt to delve into my feelings, I'd continue my rebellious approach. Ignoring what was really going on, I'd spend the day gorging myself on fattening foods and sitting like a lump in front of the television. If I had known then what I know now about the Mental Journey, I would have realized that the problem wasn't so much the fact that I took the day off. The problem was that I didn't take responsibility for my emotional state of affairs.

I'm sure this story sounds all too familiar. As everyone else does, I was ignoring the Mental Journey. Instead of focusing on the moment-to-moment experience, I was focusing on the future, and by not being in the present moment, I was creating anxiety and expectation for myself. This sets us up for failure, heartache, and disappointment. The Mental Journey teaches us to accept that the key to motivation and staying motivated is being in the here-and-now. This and this alone will enable us to remain optimistic, self-loving, and faithful to our goals. Unfortunately, just knowing this isn't going to get us motivated. Therefore I have devised a few simple mental exercises that have always assisted my Mental Journey.

TORNADO OF THOUGHTS

The biggest hindrance to becoming motivated and staying motivated is the tornado of thoughts, or the negative self-talk we all get trapped in. Negative self-talk causes us to program our thoughts with limited thinking until we accept it as the truth. We start to believe in these negative or disempowering thoughts and live our lives by them. How many times have you heard yourself say things like:

"What am I thinking? I don't have time for this today."
"I'm not disciplined; I won't stick with it."
"I've done this how many times and failed."
"I'm still tired; maybe I should have one more cup of coffee."

As members of society we have become conditioned for *pessimism* instead of *optimism*. Pessimistic thoughts seem safer than optimistic thoughts; we know what the results will be, and they feel more comfortable. Optimistic thoughts change our outlook on life and ultimately our destiny. Sure, there's much more fear in the unknown. But as author Susan Jeffers says, feeling the fear and going for it anyway will set you free.

To really release yourself from the hold of this tornado of thoughts and experience freedom for life, take a moment to consider where most of your thoughts and words originate.

To begin your journey toward positive thinking, you must learn to identify and escape disempowering thoughts.

Disempowering thoughts come from a place in us that has been educated to think that in order to survive, we have to be detached from the feelings of others. These thoughts cause us to distrust people and come from a belief that the world is out to get us. By allowing disempowering thoughts to take control, we are forgetting that every situation in our life, whether it be good or bad, can be used to empower us. Remember, the harder the struggle, the more enjoyable the reward. Disempowering thoughts are usually manifested from unhealthy conditioning and are rooted in the "good, better, best" philosophy. They often cause us to act as wounded individuals who do not trust in our ability to handle any threat that comes our way.

While confronting our tornado of thoughts, we will use techniques to empower us and our thoughts, turning disempowering thoughts around.

Empowering thoughts stem from the belief that we can handle anything that happens to us, for we are strong. They will enable us to stop seeing the world as a threat, and instead to see it as a place to learn and grow, give and shine. Empowering thoughts know that any situation, be it good or bad, can be used to enlighten us.

The truth is, we are our thoughts. What we think becomes what we say, and what we say becomes who we are. Think about how many times in the past we have conditioned ourselves to believe in the negative things we think and say. How many more times are you going to sabotage yourself with statements like "Oh, I can't do that; that isn't for me; I can't do everything; that's for someone else." I implore you, once and for all, stop. This chatter will stunt your growth and prevent you from becoming the spectacular creature that you are.

Not long ago, I knew I had entered a downright spiral, and I was determined to find a way to stop the negative thought. We have only one life on this planet, and it's not a dress rehearsal. The show must go on. So do we want to perform, or be a spectator? Do we want to take a backseat and observe the scenes passing us by? Or do we want to shine bright and vivid under that spotlight we call life? Life is for the living. So ask yourself, If you're not here, where are you? Come on, gang, follow me. I'm with you! I have created JayWalking for you, and together we can use it to give us the confidence we have lost contact with. By inhaling fresh air, singing a song, or just saying "I can" with conviction, you can begin to conquer the negativity in your life.

In order to keep myself motivated and positive, I often think of myself as an engine on a long train. Behind me I am pulling twenty-four separate storage cars, each representing the hours in my day. I have a choice to fill my boxcars with rocks or gold. My question to you is, How do you envision your cars?

I have a friend who hasn't worked in months. He is very personable, articulate, attractive, and well-read, but he has chosen to feed into his disempowering thoughts. He comes from the belief that he can't do any better. Every time I see him, he takes one look at me, and before any words come out of my mouth, he says, "I know, I know, I'm going to do it; I'm going to do something with my life. I promised myself, and I will." The problem is that this conversation has gone on for years now. He has chosen to fill his train with rocks instead of gold.

I have another friend who is a successful businesswoman. Her life hasn't been any easier than yours or mine. She has definitely had her share of difficulties. But by facing each problem head-on she has managed to fill her cars with gold. She chooses to take life moment by moment. She says that when times get challenging, she turns to her internal spirit and works on focusing on the task at hand. By focusing on her internal spirit, she has not only made herself stronger, but also more capable of taking things piece by piece instead of being overcome by the big picture.

How are you filling your cars? Remember, no matter how tough times get, and what challenges you've already faced, you always have the opportunity to fill your cars with gold.

The exercises that follow will serve to help you counteract all of your disempowering thoughts and actions through motivation, visualization, and your newly awakening self-esteem. These are the techniques that will enable you to fill your cars with gold.

POSITIVE AFFIRMATIONS

*Better than a thousand useless words
is one single word that gives peace.*

—THE BUDDHA

The first step toward replacing disempowering thoughts with empowering thoughts is positive affirmations. Positive affirmations are words, sounds, or phrases that you repeat to yourself anytime you need a momentary lift. By inserting positive affirmations into our thought routine, we begin a new conditioning process that in time will replace our tornado of thoughts with positive mind chatter. So even though the tornado may continue to whirl, it will be filled with positive reinforcement. Remember, negative thoughts are not honest thoughts; they are the imposters.

Discipline and consistency have always been challenges to me. I usually have no trouble getting myself extremely motivated for a period of time, and then I get bored and let the project slide. I think we can all relate to this one. So how do we escape the cycle of not following through?

Whenever I'm feeling a little worn, tired, and unmotivated, I come up with a positive affirmation. The personal affirmation I use frequently is "I'm recharging my batteries and enjoying the process." By stating an affirmation like this, you take all of the stress and expectancy off the moment, which allows you to progress to a more peaceful place.

Before I say any more, I'd like you to go on an adventure with me. We're going to explore the tornado of thoughts. Keep in mind that the tornado of thoughts is made up of negative, repetitive phrases and beliefs that have conditioned us to stay paralyzed from taking positive action in our lives.

EXERCISE TOUCHING THE TORNADO

Close your eyes and imagine that you have just stepped out of your body. You begin to notice your own self standing in front of you. Focus on your breathing, and as you begin to relax allow your inner resources to guide you.

Notice your hair. Its texture. How the light enhances its color. Notice the shape of your head. Your skin. Your eyes. The length of your neck. Your shoulders. Your stomach. Your hands and your legs.

As you begin to travel down your body, you will meet your tornado of thoughts, and it will be there to pass judgment on you and make you feel unacceptable. Watch how the tornado takes hold of you, taunting and confusing your focus. Listen to the negative thoughts running through your mind. Keep in mind that this is an exercise, and that you are safe as the observer, and remember, at any time you can stop this process. Notice how the destructive thoughts that begin to twist through your mind are very similar to a record playing over and over at high speed. Thoughts such as

I hate my hair.
My face looks old/tired.
This is stupid, what could I possibly learn.
I don't have the patience.
My legs are fat.

These are worn-out, self-defeating, negative thoughts. They become such a part of our mental programming that we begin to believe that they are the truth of our being. How can we possibly move freely through life with all of this clutter? And what is it ultimately doing for us? Nothing. We must stop these thoughts and initiate new, positive thoughts and emotions.

EXERCISE AFFIRMATIONS

By inserting positive affirmations into your thought routine, you slowly end your negative tornado of thoughts and replace it with a positive outlook on life and on yourself.

So how do we develop these positive affirmations? The following guidelines will help you find your personal affirmations:

Always phrase affirmations in the present tense. By saying an affirmation in the present tense, you fool the mind into thinking that the affirmation has already happened, creating a positive effect. Example: "My body, mind, and spirit radiate beautifully and fabulously right now."

Keep affirmations short, simple and tailored to you. The simpler the affirmation, the easier it is to remember. Ask yourself what you need, what you're looking for, what you want to feel, and create a powerful affirmation all your own. Affirm what you want, and not what you don't want. "I'm not late anymore" doesn't give the mind a clear image of what is expected. By changing the sentence to "Punctuality is easy and effortless," a positive image is created. It allows your mind and body to create more optimistic possibilities.

Be emotionally assertive and charismatic. When saying your affirmation, always be aware of your underlying emotional state. Having lots of passion, energy, joy, and happiness upon your verbal expression will create a much more effective anchor so you can achieve the abundance that is rightfully yours. Your personal affirmation will be more effective if you say it out loud and with a smile. However, if that feels too weird, you can just as easily keep it in your head.

While JayWalking, I love to play with affirmations. By inhaling on the first part of the phrase—*"I'm"*—and exhaling on the second—*"energized"*—I am put into a meditative rhythm. By constantly repeating this process, I release myself from the tornado of thoughts and am transported into a more productive, centered, and peaceful place. The affirmation you choose should be something you feel very strongly about. Here is a short list to get you started:

"I'm complete."
"I'm loving life."

"I'm joyous."
"I'm organized."
"I'm prosperous."
"I'm brave."
"I'm a great communicator."
"I'm right where I want to be."

Spend some time experimenting with new and exciting affirmations that will ensure you of more motivation throughout your day.

POSITIVE VISUALIZATIONS

We don't see things as they are;
we see them as we are.

—ANAÏS NIN

The mind thinks in pictures. It's not the words, ideas, or abstract thoughts that we think about when we think; it's pictures. Let me give you an example. If I asked you to close your eyes and describe to me a tree, what would you say? What appeared in your mind when your eyes were closed? Is it the shape, color, and texture of the tree or the word or concept you see? Pictures are very powerful. They stimulate the neurotransmitters in the brain that cause us to react. Imagine cutting a lemon in half: seeing the juices flowing; smelling it, noticing the sharp aroma; bringing it up to your mouth, and biting into the bitter, acidic taste. You'll begin to notice that your mouth will salivate just as you're visualizing. This is because the subconscious mind doesn't know the difference between what is real and what is imagined.

Visualization is the process of picturing or seeing in your mind the images of people, objects, or events you want to create in your life. Your visualizations—or imagined pictures—create an intangible energy which becomes an active, living reality. This will be the most powerful mental technique you will use in my program, for it has the ability to transform your thoughts into substance.

When choosing your visualizations, always come from a place of enthusiasm. Don't criticize the area in your life that you want to change, for criticism will weigh down your creative energies and cause the visualization to lose its power. By coming from a place of love and nurturing, you will become the master of your visualization and control its ultimate destiny.

Below is a list of steps you should take to create powerful, positive visualizations. In order for this technique to work effectively, you must be in a relaxed, receptive state. I recommend that this technique be done with no external distractions. Turn the telephone off, close the appointment book, and lock yourself in a room—only then will you be able to create quiet time. Make this commitment to yourself, for you deserve the rewards.

EXERCISE MAGICAL MOMENTS

Place yourself in a relaxed position. This will help you bring in positive energies from your surroundings and make your visualizations much clearer. I find using a common yoga position works best for me. Lie on your back with your feet separated, about twelve to twenty-four inches apart. Your arms should be placed alongside your body, with palms facing the sky. If this is not comfortable for you, use whatever you find fits your personality best.

Slow your breathing gradually. Focusing on your breathing will get you into an alpha state, relaxed and receptive. It will calm your body and bring down your heart rate. Slowly inhale and exhale, releasing the tension, and feel your body melting deeper and deeper into the floor. Breathing is the most important aspect of the visualization, because it taps into your spiritual center. While continuing your breathing, become aware of the loving, spiritual quality within you. (If you don't have a particular spiritual belief, focus on the simple things that make you happy—a wonderful piece of music, a child's smile, the greeting you receive from your pet.) By tapping into your spiritual center, you will bring yourself to a place of serenity, peace, and power.

Focus your visualization on choosing what you truly desire. You should feel a spark of enthusiasm. If you don't feel enthusiastic about your choice, focus on your breathing and allow your instinct to guide you to your next desire. Be honest with yourself. Don't force yourself to feel enthusiastic if you don't. Be specific with your desire. The subconscious can only react to what you visualize.

When visualizing, act as though your visualization is already yours, as though you are in the scene right now. This takes courage and trust.

PUTTING YOUR LIFE INTO ACTION

Joy's soul lies in the doing.

—SHAKESPEARE

How do you spell relief? Can you fill in the blank?

You probably answered "R.O.L.A.I.D.S." For years advertisers have been conditioning us to respond like Pavlov's dog to the ringing of a bell. They may repeat a slogan over and over again, like "Coke is it," or they may visually entice us with an ever-popular drum-beating pink bunny that marches across the TV screen with a battery pack attached to its back. Whatever the case, the advertisers are hopping—oops, hoping—to condition us to buy their product. No matter what we may do in our everyday lives, if the conditioning is done well, we may never forget the product or the slogan.

In advertising, the goal is to sell, and the urge to buy is not created by what you see, but how it makes you feel. When advertisers present a product, they make certain to do so at the height of a specific emotional feeling. Think of how many commercials you have seen where the setting is uplifting and fun; this is meant to bring you the viewer into a state of happiness, so you'll equate the product with enjoyment.

Commercials are not unlike many other aspects of our lives. If we experience happiness while eating French fries, hot apple pies, and vanilla shakes, we often equate happiness with eating fast food.

To see beyond this scheme, we have to realize that we're creatures of habit, and that all of these rituals we create for ourselves are hard to get out of.

Let's say you're JayWalking down a quiet, suburban street, the sun is shining, the birds are singing, and you're feeling on top of the world. You haven't picked up a fattening piece of food for more than a week. Feeling optimistic, confident, and secure, you suddenly turn a corner and see your favorite fast-food restaurant.

What are you thinking now? I'm sure it's not about the birds singing, the sun shining, and that serene suburban street. Oh no. It's that big paper bag filled with extra large fries, a few hamburgers, and a thick creamy shake.

You see, it's inevitable. If the conditioning is repeated over and over again, we will never forget it. Now, wouldn't it be fabulous if at any given moment in our lives we could take action to stop eating fatty foods, or tell our boss we want a raise, or feel great and energized and get up off our chair to JayWalk. Well, I'm here to tell you I can help you take that action and stop the procrastination in all areas of your life.

Before you can get started on the positive aspects of your life, you need to rid yourself of negative energy. I believe that the true reason we want to partake in a fitness program is not to create a sculpted, lean body, but to achieve a different emotional state. As advertisers, we too have conditioned ourselves to have negative images of ourselves. JayWalking is beneficial in part because our focus becomes emotional, not material. Think for a moment about all the material things you desire. Is it really the things themselves that will make you happy or the emotional state you believe you will achieve by having them? Advertising would like us to believe that it is the things themselves, when really what we are trying to change is our emotions.

Emotions are very powerful. They can either propel you to ultimate success or paralyze you in fear. The exercise that follows may be extremely uncomfortable; however, it is important that you take the time to truly feel the emotional pains and pleasures that exist within you. Emotions will become your fuel to propel you into a future of unlimited possibilities.

EXERCISE BACKING INTO THE FUTURE

Let's imagine for a moment that you are sitting in the ultimate time machine. This vehicle has the ability to take you anywhere your wishes command, at any given moment. As you sit in the vehicle, look around you. You become transfixed by an intricate control panel. And directly to the right of the steering wheel you see a time gauge with bright red, flashing numbers and letters. What's flashing is the exact date and time of this very moment.

Here I'd like you to get out a pen or marker, preferably red, and *write down the date and time.* _____ This date, this moment, will have an indelible impact on the rest of your life.

Now that you've filled in today's date and time, you have made a commitment—a commitment that will change your life. We are going to take that time machine for a ride. Remember, you are the driver in control of your destiny. I am by your side, just observing the journey.

Okay, let's get a move on! The trip is about to begin. You should *set the time machine to the same date and time, five years in the past.* Slowly place the car in reverse and put your foot on the accelerator. You begin to see your life flash in front of you; it's like a blur, but you're amazed that you can remember and see all of the poignant details. Your visualization techniques are invaluable here. Suddenly, the machine comes to an abrupt stop. You see the exhaust fumes clearing from the front of the windshield, and there you see yourself on this very day, five years in the past.

Now I'm going to give you a list of questions. When answering these questions, keep in mind that writing down the words that express your emotional state is extremely important. Keep them simple and to the point. Each of these words will give you a clearer sense of why you are the way you are. Emotions can tie us down or set us free.

An example: What New Year's resolutions did you make in the past that you threw out the window? *I promised myself I'd work out three times a week and didn't.*

How did that make you feel? *Weak, sad, doubtful, tired, unconfident.*

How did that make you look? *It made me look tense, haggard, and confused.*

What did that decision do for you? *It caused me to gain ten pounds within the year and created a chronic knee problem because of the excess weight.*

Answer the following questions and be as honest as possible. Keep in mind that the purpose of this exercise is for you to truly feel the emotions behind the questions. Spend some time to really recreate the past moments and don't be afraid to feel the uncomfortable emotional states. This process may be very difficult. Don't be afraid to take a break if you feel you need one. *Remember you are answering the questions as they applied five years ago.* Observe yourself from the safe confines of your time machine and answer truthfully.

1. *What New Year's resolutions did you make in the past that you threw out the window?*
   How did that make you feel?
   How did that make you look? (See it in your face.)
   What did that decision do for you?

2. *Who did your partner/family/friend speak highly of, if not you?*
   How did that make you feel?
   How did that make you look?
   What did that decision do for you?

3. *Who were the influential people you could have met and chose not to?*
   How did that make you feel?
   How did that make you look?
   What did that decision do for you?

4. *What did the "Joneses" have that you don't have?*
   How did that make you feel?
   How did that make you look?
   What did that decision do for you?

5. *If you have children, who did they look up to, if not you?*
   How did that make you feel?
   How did that make you look?
   What did that decision do for you?

Now that you've completed work on the past, it is time to take a step toward the future. *Set that time gauge for the same date and time, five years into the future.* Trust your instincts to answer the following questions based on how you imagine you'll feel. Put that shift into drive and let's move on!

We are now hurtling into the future, faster and faster. As you feel yourself pushing back into the seat, you begin to see a blurry picture of your future, kind of like a tapestry of watercolors. You can't seem to make out exact figures or shapes, and then suddenly we come to a stop. We have arrived—five years into the future.

1. *Now that you're older, what has changed in your life?*
   How are you feeling?
   What do you look like?
   What are you doing in your life?

Now let's try going ten years into the future.

2. *What hasn't changed in your life?*
   How do you feel?
   How do you look?
   Where is your life (financially, spiritually, physically, emotionally, and socially)?

Remember that while answering these questions it is important to take the time to really feel the feelings. Look closely at yourself. Where are you? What are you doing?

Let's go again! Twenty years into the future!

What has this limited thinking cost you in your life?

Do this as many times as you feel necessary, until you really feel you are prepared to take action, to change your attitudes and outlook on life. The best part is that none of this has happened yet. The past doesn't equal the future; you still have the power to change!

When you feel comfortable that you have mastered the time machine, it is time to return to the present. Now with your new frame of mind, answer the following questions:

1. *What actions have you taken in the last month that you're proud of?*
   How did that make you feel?
   What was the look on your face?
   How did you carry your body?
   What was your energy level like? (Feel it.)

2. *What have you done for others in the past month that has helped make you a better person?*
   How did that make you feel?
   What was the look on your face?
   How did you carry your body?
   What was your energy level like?

3. *What small goals, dreams, resolutions, and promises have you had in the last month that have come true?*
   How did that make you feel?
   What was the look on your face?
   How did you carry your body?
   What was your energy level like?

Now go into the future again and look at how much you've changed your life.

Congratulations! You have successfully completed your time travel. It is now time to enjoy the rewards of your committed focus.

Take a good long look at yourself. How do you feel? Look at your face: Is it glowing with accomplishment? What are your relationships like now? Can you see how much more fully you can share your life with others?

You now have the leverage you need to take the first step in truly beginning your JayWalking program. You now realize that a healthy body begins with a positive emotional state.* When you enter the *Physical Journey*, you will now have acquired exercises that will help you to walk in confidence.

---

*For more information on taking action read Anthony Robbins's *Awaken the Giant Within*.

STOP

Slow and steady wins the race.

—AESOP

When we get up in the morning, we open our eyes, we think, Not another day of work! We brush our teeth, we think, Darn, it's only Tuesday, we comb our hair, we get in the car, and we go to work. It's all routine. It's become so routine we're not even aware of what's going on in the moment. The problem with these routines is that they're not serving our highest good. Now, wouldn't it be great if we could interrupt any of the negative patterns in our routine, find the wonder in the moment and never go back to the negative thoughts?

Think of your negative routines as a record spinning endlessly in your mind. In order to STOP the record from spinning, all you have to do is scratch it a couple of times. Now you've interrupted the negative pattern and the record will never play the same way again. You are now able to go on to more productive actions.

In the STOP technique we will create interruptions that will help you jump-start your way to healthier living, so you'll never go back to unhealthy patterns again.

The STOP technique should be performed whenever you find yourself falling into negative patterns: not going for your JayWalk, reaching for fatty foods, oversleeping, procrastinating. If you perform this exercise correctly, nothing will ever STOP you from doing it.

EXERCISE TAKING ACTION AGAIN

In the STOP technique, we use either a physical movement, a verbal sound, or a visual picture to counteract a negative pattern or action. It is important to pick a movement, sound, or picture that will give you a positive feeling. This is a very simple exercise to use when you find yourself falling into one of those negative patterns.

Start out by making a list of funny or energetic moments in your past. Choose events that made you feel energized or made you laugh out loud. Then go beyond that moment and try to remember the people involved in the situation. Focus on colors, sounds you may have heard, or any distinctive smells you may have encountered. Do this exercise with a smile on your face, grinning from ear to ear. (Oh, go ahead, no one is watching.)

How are you feeling? This is one exercise that always makes me chuckle. It is amazing to me that all those sounds, sights, and feelings are still so fresh, alive, and ready to make me laugh.

Once you make a list of funny situations and truly feel the emotions, you are ready to link them to your subconscious.

Choose a physical movement that is very unique, something you don't normally do. In other words, you don't want to use the crossing of your legs or the blinking of an eye. They happen too often in day-to-day life to be effective for the STOP technique. I like to tap the side of my cheek three times or pound on my chest like a gorilla.

Now think back to one of your funny or exhilarating situations. Remember to choose a situation in which you feel an intense amount of energy. Maybe you just made the final dip on a super-speed roller coaster, and you're feeling tingly, fresh, and transformed. Or you caught a bus that was just about to pull away, and you're amazed by the surge of energy your body has created.

Whatever the event was, make sure you're feeling that peak level of energy. Recapture the moment vividly, using all of your imagination and senses. *The key is to feel the emotions, and at the height of the emotional feeling—laughter, energy, exhilaration—do your physical movement.* For example, as the roller coaster completes its final descent, I pound my chest like a gorilla. I recommend that you link this emotion with your physical movement at least fifteen times, over and over again: *Feel emotions, do the physical movement. Feel emotions, do the physical movement. Feel emotions, do the physical movement. . . .*

You will be amazed at the results. Be aware that you will feel a peak level of energy when performing this technique, so the more specific and detailed you are with the STOP technique, the more success you will achieve.

EXERCISE SUPER GLUING

> *One ought, every day at least, to hear a little song,*
> *read a good poem, see a fine picture, and if at all possible,*
> *to speak a few reasonable words.*
>
> —GOETHE

You should now be a professional at getting yourself into a peak emotional state—one of laughter, energy, and exhilaration. But in order to make the STOP technique effective, we have to make it stick. We could consider the Super Gluing technique as an additional boost to STOP. The amazing thing about the Super Gluing technique is that it's nothing new for you. People do it all the time.

Think about listening to your favorite music. Music is a very strong anchor that can automatically put you into a certain emotional state. No matter how you're feeling, just playing the music can transport you to a completely new level.

Let's take another example. Does the smell of a certain fragrance remind you of any particular event? I know that for me, the smell of chocolate chip cookies baking in an oven brings back the warm, comforting feeling of my aunt's house in the fall. Anything that is repeated over and over when you are in a peak emotional state will become anchored. It will stick like glue.

The following steps will help you super glue your STOP technique so that at any given point in your JayWalk you can fire up.

1. Imagine yourself sitting in an empty theater watching the movie of your negative beliefs.
2. Enhance this picture with color, sound, texture, and movement.
3. Now imagine you are holding onto a paddle with a little rubber ball attached by a rubber string.
4. Place a small, stamplike picture of your ideal self fulfilling all your dreams on the ball.
5. Lift the paddle up over your head and bounce the ball off the paddle, aiming it at the screen. Watch how the ball gets closer and closer to the movie screen, until it hits and explodes the screen, erasing the old movie and bringing to life the ideal you.
6. The trick is to hit that ball onto that screen twenty times and with each and every strike shout "Yes!" as loud as you can. Feel how amazing the ideal you can be.

Do this exercise three times a day for three days so that you'll feel so fabulous you'll be "stuck" on the ideal you.

THE HERE AND NOW

One's ship comes in over a calm sea.

—FLORENCE SCOVELL SHINN

Until you picked up this book jaywalking was something you tried to avoid, or at least do away from the watchful eyes of police officers. The irony here is that when we jaywalk we are thinking and acting haphazardly. Isn't that what we do quite often—let our minds run rampant, thereby not enjoying the moment?

Whether we act like it or not, we live in the here and now. This is the only moment we will ever know, and all too often we don't take advantage of that. Take note of just how often you fall into a mechanical way of life, a "back to the ol' grind," Monday-morning type of feeling. It seems as if our lives are on automatic pilot, with no one at the helm. We don't even know who's doing the doing anymore.

We allow these moments in our lives, where our true power lies, to overwhelm us. We lose contact with our creativity, our uniqueness—what makes us us. If we're not careful, those foggy moments begin to dominate our lives.

In order to find a balance within ourselves, we must first learn to pay more attention to this very moment. It is the only place where we will feel power, growth, and change. Putting our energies on planning breakfast or dinner when it's lunchtime puts a lot of undue stress on our lives.

So, gang, it is time for us to redefine the concept of jaywalking. We're going to have some fun. We are going to bring some light to the word. We're going to make it legal, fun, stressless, and healthy.

Mindfulness, stillness, prayer, meditation, conditioning—these are all words to explain how you can focus your mind to experience the here and now. The Here and Now is an exercise to train the mind to create more peace so that we can use that peace in each moment we experience life. In the here and now, there is no stress. In the here and now, time is not running us. In the here and now, we have no concerns for an outcome, because we are truly enjoying the journey. If your mind is not centered here, it is more than likely not going to be centered when you arrive in the next moment. Being in the here and now has definitely been my guiding angel to all of life's challenges.

Destined to learn more on this insightful topic, I began my research to find out how being in the here and now could benefit me on my fitness and health program. I found remarkable results. Living your life in the moment can reduce the severity of chronic pain; individuals who are in the here and now have less anxiety and depression; anger and hostility can be released, insomnia reduced, and healthier sleeping patterns initiated. Women who live in the here and now experience a 60 percent decrease in the severity of PMS symptoms, and patients with cancer and AIDS experience a decrease in symptoms.

Just think: If the here and now creates such remarkable benefits to our health and well-being, imagine incorporating a spectacular walking routine into this process. The results could be phenomenal.

Use the following exercises to assist you in experiencing being in the here and now. The exercises are beneficial in creating a sense of peace and balance and are a wonderful addition to your walking program.

EXERCISE A MORSEL AND MORE

If you bring forth what is within you,
what you bring forth will save you.

—GOSPEL OF THOMAS

Recently I volunteered my services to train a group of marathon walkers. A week prior to the event, I had been searching for just the right speech to motivate my team for the grueling 26.2-mile course. As I sat at my kitchen table, chewing on a handful of grapes, it dawned on me: *Food!*

Food brought me into the moment! Blocking out all distractions, I began to go on a journey with the handful of grapes I had been holding. I then shared this technique with the group and told them that this process could connect them with their internal power. Using a small morsel of food, I've laid out the steps to establish this technique.

1. Choose a small morsel of food, preferably something you enjoy eating.

2. Get yourself relaxed in a quiet place.

3. Take a close look at your morsel.
   Focus on the color. (Does it have different tones?)
   If you are holding it, how does it feel in your hand?
   If it is on a spoon or fork, what type of texture does it have (smooth/rough)?

4. Slowly bring the food to your nose.
   Does it have a distinctive aroma?
   Do you notice your mouth beginning to water?
   How does your body feel?

5. Begin to chew on the morsel. Notice how it disperses in your mouth.
   Does it stay together or break apart?
   Does the flavor become more, or less, enhanced?
   Does it stick to your teeth or the roof of your mouth?

Notice how by focusing on your food you were transported to a new perception of the moment. This exercise should have helped you experience the now, instead of being preoccupied with what you were going to do next, and what you want to have happen.

THE BREATHING LIGHT

Life's but breath.

—SHAKESPEARE

Breathing is the bridge that connects our body to our mind and spirit. In essence, breathing gives us life. In each breath we cleanse the system, bringing oxygen to the blood. The oxygen activates the lymphatic system, which releases toxins. By using proper breathing techniques, we can improve the lymphatic system's efficiency. It is a proven fact that with proper breathing we can lead a more productive, vigorous life.

The way we breathe sets off many facets to our world: our mental capacity to think, our physical capacity to move, and our emotional capacity to feel. Our breathing is our natural, built-in tranquilizer. If used correctly, breathing can help us achieve soothing, calming, healthy effects. Breathing exercises are especially good when you're walking, for they can calm and lower your heart rate if you begin to get out of breath, and give you more energy if you need that extra get up and go.

Take a moment to notice how you breathe. If you are feeling tense, you may be breathing from your chest, rather than from your diaphragm. Breathing from your chest keeps your mind and body in a state of chronic stress. Diaphragmatic breathing creates the opposite effect, allowing your body to become relaxed, calm, and in control. Breathe deep!

BREATHING EXERCISE #1

1. Place your hand on your upper chest and take deep breaths. (If your hand rises, you're breathing incorrectly.)
2. Place your other hand below the rib cage. Inhale slowly, and imagine your stomach expanding with air, like a balloon being blown up. Your upper chest should stay flat. Focus on making your breath as even and steady as possible.
3. Exhale and imagine the body relaxing, releasing all of its tension, and allowing the stress to dissipate through your breathing.

4. Inhale on four counts. Hold for sixteen counts (to oxygenate blood). Release on eight counts (to remove toxins).

Repeat this exercise periodically throughout the day.

BREATHING EXERCISE #2

1. Find a quiet, tranquil place. Begin to focus on your breathing.
2. Notice that your breathing has a rhythm all its own. It needs no direction. It instinctually knows what to do.
3. Begin to notice the path your breathing takes. Do you inhale through your nose and exhale through your mouth? Follow the air as it goes into your nose and down through the back of your throat, watching your lungs expand to the top and exhaling the air up your windpipe and through your mouth.
4. Begin to notice the sensations that your breath has on its path. Is it cool when you inhale? Warm when you exhale? How do your lungs feel when they're full? How do they feel when they're empty? Do you feel the air passing through your lips or rushing up your nose?

All of these sensations bring you into the present moment, where your true power lies. Experiment and create your own unique journey.

EXERCISE BODY SCANNING

Some day the inner light will shine forth from us,
and then we shall need no other light.

—GOETHE

The Body Scanning technique is much like the breathing exercises. It allows us to experience or follow a path.

This exercise is another technique to bring you into the here and now. It will help get you connected to and become more familiar with your physical body. This is a great exercise to try in the morning when you begin your JayWalk. It will wake up all of your body parts.

1. Imagine a bright, vivid light, radiating at the top of your head. Become aware of its color and shape. Gold, silver, and white are the most powerful, for they symbolize spirituality, cleansing, and purity.
2. Slowly begin to follow the light as it radiates through the top of your head, awakening your hair follicles and permeating the center of your brain.
3. Continue to follow this light, and notice how its path begins to relax all of your muscle groups (neck, shoulders, upper back, chest, lower back, buttocks, hips, legs, ankles, and toes). Be aware of where you are holding tension, and notice the power of the light. You may want to radiate the light into your internal organs if you are experiencing any internal problems.
4. Once the light has enveloped your whole body, absorb the sensations, keeping yourself focused on one area, such as your heart, stomach, or lungs—this will give you a calming place to go and will keep you focused if your tornado of thoughts should get in the way. Allow this experience to bring you to a new level.

You now have all of the motivation and determination you need to proceed to the next stage in *JayWalking: The Ultimate Fitness Journey*. Remember, whenever your tornado of thoughts gets to you, just tap into any one of the exercises from the Mental Journey.

STRESS MANAGEMENT TECHNIQUES

Exercise is a great stress reducer. However, exercise alone cannot take care of our mental state of affairs. Therefore I have collected a series of very powerful and effective stress management techniques that can help you achieve a sense of balance and well-being in your life. The stress management techniques should be introduced toward the middle or end of your program. Then you can give way to what's in store without feeling you still have physical work to do. Don't get me wrong, I'm not against applying stress management techniques at any given point in your JayWalk. If you've had a stressful day or week, it may be wise to start your program with these techniques so that you can get yourself focused and receptive to the physical and emotional benefits, and then walk with greater success.

The best place to perform the following technique is in a quiet, secluded setting, such as a wooded area, a lake, around a bed of flowers, or along the ocean. Anyplace that is away from crowds and distracting sounds. If you decide to walk with a partner or group, I would highly recommend that this section be committed to quiet time. That means no talking for those of you chatty Cathys. *Sssshhh!*

One day during a JayWalking class, I was disturbed by the piercing sound of a siren as a rescue squad rushed by. I began to realize that beyond the screeching sound was actually a beautiful note. This usually annoying sound became rather meditative. I shared this concept with the class and to my amazement, they all agreed with me. I decided to use that realization and take the time in my life more often to hear that beyond the ordinary is the extraordinary.

Sounds can take us to a whole new level in our JayWalking program. Active listening is the state in which we are truly listening to tones and rhythms, which create an increased calorie burn. Focusing on sounds of nature creates a tranquil escape from one's everyday routine. As you begin to cool down from your JayWalking fitness journey, begin to focus on the sounds of the environment. Notice the sounds that are closer to you and your reactions to them. And then step back for a moment and begin to notice the sounds farther away. How far can your hearing expand? To what extent can you hear nature at work? For even more of a challenge listen to the sounds of your body. Your breathing, and heart beat. The sounds you make when you swallow or cough. Whenever you have any type of distracting thought, refocus on the sounds. This will bring you into the here and now, clear your mind, and open you up to the wonders of your keen sense of hearing.

As you learned earlier, color creates a mood, setting us up for a state of passion or cool quiet. Another great stress releaser is to focus on the color of nature. As you begin to cool down, notice the different colors—not just superficially, but making note of the details. Try focusing on one leaf of a tree. Notice how the color on that one leaf has many different shades of green. Or focus on a flower and notice how each petal has independent colors, even though as a whole the flower may appear to be all one color. Be careful to notice how each color you focus on creates a different emotional shift. How do you feel when you look at the colors of a bright green tree? Or the colors in a vibrant bed of flowers? Again, do not let your mind wander; and if it should, bring it back to the vibrancy of color. This way you're sure to be in the here and now.

During the end of your JayWalking program you may notice a feeling of euphoria. This is due to the intense amount of oxygen your body has absorbed. This feeling will enhance your ability to observe the world in a whole new light. You'll be more centered and calm, but still extremely aware of how your thoughts are far more creative and less urgent. Imagine for a moment how your life would be with this wonderful new state. How would you view the world, your work, friends, family, the clouds in the sky, or even the fresh air!

Have fun with this, and don't pass any judgment. Become that child at play.

JayWalker: How do stress management techniques differ from here-and-now exercises?

Jay: These two sections are very much the same. They are designed to allow you to change your perception of what you are seeing. This brings you into the moment, where your true power lies. In this moment, you are able to see the world as a safe and nurturing place.

JayWalker: Will JayWalking release me from judgment?

Jay: When we judge others, it is a reflection of our own level of insecurity. How can we accept others' weaknesses, mistakes, and flaws, if we cannot accept our own? The more we find fault in others, the more unsure we are about ourselves. In order to give up this unproductive thought process, ask yourself, What about that person could I like? Watch as that one choice begins to radiate and grow. You'll begin to see the good unveiled, and then you can accept and let others be. With this small shift you can become encouraging to others.

JayWalker: Will JayWalking get me out of a depression?

Jay: Depression exists when we feed into the negative aspects of the tornado of thoughts. It is the belief that we have begun to match the negative expectations we have created for ourselves and the world. We become depressed when we are not encouraged, reinforced, and taught to believe in ourselves.

THE PHYSICAL JOURNEY

A journey of a thousand miles must begin with a single step.

—LAO TZU

One day after JayWalking in New York's Central Park, I began to pay careful attention to the number of people working out. I noticed bicyclers, runners, walkers, and Rollerbladers. As I observed further, I noticed that very few of these people actually looked as if they were enjoying what they were doing. Huffing and puffing with pained looks on their faces, they trudged along on their workout. Why would these people want to do something that made them that miserable?

I decided to make it my mission to find out why people work out. I found most of the answers very astonishing. One woman said, "If I don't, I couldn't stand to look at myself."

Other comments included "Because it's what everyone who is anybody is doing," and "My girlfriend will find me more attractive," and "If I don't, I'll start to look older than I am."

No wonder people don't enjoy their workout. If these are some of the reasons why you are working out, or why you avoid working out, then it is definitely time for you to start JayWalking. In the Physical Journey you will gain a higher appreciation for walking, and exercise. You will find that the actual movement and mechanics of walking bring up stored emotions and feelings from your subconscious mind that you weren't even aware you had. Most importantly, you will begin to build a relationship with your body that you didn't even know existed. You will begin to really focus on the way your body feels and moves, and what its needs are. You will uncover feelings and emotions that make you fit as opposed to feelings that make you sit.

By combining the Physical Journey with some of the techniques you have already learned in the Mental Journey, you will be able to bring yourself immediately into the moment. This is one of the main reasons people are unable to enjoy their workout. Most of the people I interviewed in the park were working out in fear. Their belief was that they would find happiness in a perfect body; they weren't even thinking of their whole person. As we learned in the *Mental Journey,* you won't truly enjoy yourself, or your life, if you aren't living in the here and now. The person who is truly going to enjoy a workout, the person who has a calm about him or her, is the person who lives in the moment. Being in the here and now means enjoying your exercise at the moment. Instead of focusing on losing the weight by Thanksgiving or fitting into a new bathing suit by the Fourth of July, the commitment to being in the moment activates the process of trust. Learning to trust is how we release the fear in wanting to have a perfect body.

Remember what you learned in the Mental Journey; being physically fit is not enough. It is wonderful to imagine what our lives would be like if our bodies were perfectly symmetrical: broad shoulders, firm chest, cinched waist, long sculpted legs, and don't forget that tight perky butt. But let's face it, gang, that's just an ideal. We have been conditioned to believe that happiness and beauty lie in a beautifully fit, chiseled body. I'm here to tell you that it's baloney. It may be perceived that way, but the truth lies beneath the surface, under those layers, where you find the true resources of yourself.

Learning to become physically fit involves learning to become mentally fit first. That is why it is very important that you have completed the Mental Journey before you embark on the Physical Journey. I can't stress how much of a difference this will make to your whole experience.

In the Physical Journey, you will learn that being physically fit takes far less time than vacuuming the living room, washing the kitchen floor, or scrubbing the bathroom tub. All in all, the Physical

Journey will enhance the quality of your life and put that spring back into your step. Keep in mind that combining the Mental and Spiritual Journeys in your JayWalk will make you a more well-rounded individual. In the Physical Journey, you will learn how to construct your own JayWalking program to achieve ultimate physical fitness benefits from five minutes to an hour-plus a day.

WHY EXERCISE?

If the Mental Journey is going to make you a better and happier person, why even bother with physical exercise?

In July of 1996, **the Surgeon General released a report stating that lack of physical activity is detrimental to your health.** This monumental statement hit the health and fitness industry like a bombshell. For the first time ever the government stated *in no uncertain terms* that "without exercise you are going to wind up with health problems."

The report advises sedentary persons to accumulate thirty minutes of moderately intense exercise per day, such as walking for fifteen minutes twice a day. By moderate-intensity exercise, they mean walking at about three to four miles per hour.

This is wonderful news for all you JayWalkers out there! Five minutes here, ten minutes there: It all adds up.

This report is not meant to discourage you avid exercisers to stop what you've been doing, but rather to get you to realize that with exercise, sometimes less is more. Adding a JayWalk to your weekly high-intensity fitness regimen could be extremely beneficial in achieving a sound mind as well as a sound body.

WARM-UP

If there is one thing that every fitness book in the world has in common, it's this: the *warm-up*! Yes, I know, you've become so excited after reading this book that you just can't wait to lace up your sneakers and hit the road. I commend your spirit; however, without a proper warm-up you're placing yourself at a high risk for muscle tears and fatigue. I also recommend that before embarking on any fitness program, you consult with your physician for the A-OK.

A warm-up increases your heart rate, your body temperature, blood flow, and mental activity, and preps your muscles to move. When warming up, your body starts to release a natural lubricant called synovial fluid (or "joint oil"), which adds mobility to your joints for less muscle fatigue and greater movement in your stride.

I have designed a series of effective warm-up stretches specifically for JayWalking. While JayWalking, or doing any kind of exercise, it is important to keep in mind that a good warm-up should be no fewer than three to five minutes. Use a full range of motion and don't lock your joints. Mentally focus on the muscles that are being stretched, and whatever you do, *do not bounce*. Bouncing can cause tearing in muscle fiber! Keep a slow and steady rhythmic movement.

Remember with all these exercises, that once you do one side you need to then do the other.

HAMSTRING STRETCH

The hamstrings, the quadriceps, the calves, and the buttocks are the muscles most utilized in JayWalking.

The hamstring muscle is located on the back of the leg from the base of the buttocks to the back of the knee, and serves to flex and rotate the leg, and to extend the thigh. This stretch is very important for proper flexibility.

Position: Stand upright. Place your feet shoulder-width apart. Lean slightly forward, bend both knees and lean into left hip, resting your hands above your left knee and extending your right leg directly in front of you. Think of an imaginary thread attached to the base of your spine and pulling your buttocks to the sky. Keep your chin lifted and your shoulders back, and open up your chest.

Movement: Point and flex the right foot to feel the stretch in the hamstrings and the calf. *Repeat this*

Hamstring Stretch

movement 10 to 15 times and then switch to your other leg. Reminder: Keep your feet shoulder-width apart to help your balance. Keep your back straight when stretching. Keep in mind that this stretch is responsible for the main push-off in our walking motion.

QUADRICEPS STRETCH

The quadricep muscles are some of the largest muscles in the lower body. They run from the front of the hip all the way down to the top of the knee. They are responsible for giving you strength to perform uphill climbing, squats, and stair walking. JayWalking can work wonders on this muscle group.

Position: To warm up your quads properly, stand upright and place your left hand onto a park bench, tree, or fence for support. Then bend your right knee behind you and hold onto your right foot or ankle.

Movement: Perform 10 to 15 gentle swinging movements in a forward and backward motion. Focus on feeling the front of your right leg stretching. Repeat on your left leg. Try to keep the supporting leg slightly bent and *avoid leaning your upper body forward.*

Quadriceps Stretch

ALTERNATE QUADRICEPS STRETCH

If balance is a problem on the quad stretch, this alternative is very effective. While standing upright, extend your left leg slightly in front of your right (don't cross the legs), reaching back with your right leg. Tilt your pelvis slightly forward and slowly bend the right knee to ground, move up and down, then return to the upright position. Be careful to go straight down with the back knee, but don't touch it all the way to the ground. Always keep the front knee directly above the ankle to avoid injury.

Alternate Quadriceps Stretch

TOTAL BACK STRETCH

The lower back is the most important muscle group. I recommend warming it up on a daily basis, even if you aren't exercising. It's also where most of us hold tension and repressed emotions. With this stretch, we can free ourselves from physical discomfort and emotional baggage.

Position: Stand upright. Place your feet shoulder-width apart. Keeping your knees slightly bent, lean your upper body forward, so your back is flat. Place your hands above your knees to support your upper body, and keep your chin lifted **See position 1.**

Movement: Tilt your pelvis forward, tucking your buttocks under yourself, creating a "Hunchback of Notre Dame" effect. Repeat the movement 10 to 15 times, tilting your pelvis forward and backward. **See position 2.**

Total Back Stretch—Position 1   *Total Back Stretch—Position 2*

UPPER BACK STRETCH

Like the lower back, the upper back is another storage bin for physical and emotional tension. Along with proper stretching exer-

Upper Back Stretch #1

Upper Back Stretch #2

cises and breathing techniques, this movement is the perfect tension tamer. It is excellent for opening the chest and developing proper postural alignment.

Position: Standing up straight and tall, feet shoulder width apart, extend both your arms out to the side of your body at shoulder level.

Movement: Keeping your arms straight and extended, gently swing them forward and back as though you were applauding. Cross arms in front of chest and then open arms back out to side.

HEAD TILT

Adding mobility to the neck is the last step for a proper warm-up. Stand in a comfortable, upright position, feet shoulder-width apart, shoulders back, chest slightly lifted, and abdominals held in. Gently tilt your head from shoulder to shoulder, reaching

Head Tilt

your ear toward your shoulder and alternating from the right side to the left side For variety, you may roll the chin to the chest, in a semi-circle alternating sides from right to left. Tilt right and left about ten times slowly.

STAGES OF JAYWALKING

LEVEL 1: THE STRIDE

This is the beginning stage of your new JayWalking program and will teach you the proper techniques.

Walking is a natural movement. It is something we do every day, and unlike running, it is something we were made to do. Therefore, I'm going to avoid getting too complex about proper walking technique and how one should walk. Instead I'm going to show you the proper technique to make your walk more effective. Remember: In JayWalking, there is no wrong—everything is right.

As with everything in JayWalking, you can gain certain benefits from practicing the Stride. It can help

Reduce stress
Increase oxygen uptake
Decrease anxiety
Improve sleep patterns
Increase positive thoughts
Decrease risk of osteoporosis
Decrease/eliminate lower back pain

WALKING TECHNIQUE

Position: Stand comfortably with your feet shoulder-width apart and your chin lifted. Imagine that your head is a helium-filled balloon, all of your body parts following the gentle lift of the balloon, the neck, shoulders, trunk, legs, and feet all lifting effortlessly to the sky. Don't try to make anything happen, just relax and enjoy the lightness and the sensations of your body.

Movement: Slowly rock your body forward and back. Then increase the momentum. Notice how your weight shifts from the front to the back of your foot. When you feel the need to catch your weight, bring one foot forward. You now have your natural walking stride. Begin to walk. Do not overstride: overstriding will slow you down.

Arms: Allow your arms to dangle along the trunk of your body. Begin to swing them forward and back in a scissorlike fashion, alternating arms. Follow the natural rhythm of your body. Feel the circulation in your fingertips begin to increase. Notice how the arms cascade along your body, like the pendulum of a clock. Take

Walking Technique #1

the time to notice any other sensations you may be feeling in this movement. How do your shoulders feel? Your legs? Your neck? Just keep walking.

Feet: Begin to concentrate on flexing your foot. Each time you bring your leg forward, slightly lift your big toe up to your knee, and at the same time dig your heel into the ground. If you are performing this movement correctly, it should feel a little awkward. By flexing your foot you begin to increase the stretch in your calf (the lower part of your leg). There's no need to overflex the foot in Level 1.

The whole point of this technique is to work all the muscles in your legs. With each step the calf, hamstrings, and buttocks stretch

SHIN MAINTENANCE

If you continue to feel discomfort in your shins during your JayWalk, it is a good possibility that you are flexing your foot too much and overemphasizing your heel strike. Don't try so hard. Instead, think of rolling through the foot. When your foot is behind you, gently push your toes into the ground. This will ease the pain in your shins by stretching them. With each step it should be as if you are pointing your foot behind you and giving your shin a stretch. In every movement, when one muscle stretches, the opposite contracts. So if the front of your leg is feeling tight, then the back of your leg is being stretched.

After about twenty minutes of walking, most of my students get accustomed to the initial shin discomfort of JayWalking. The body will become warmer, and you'll be able to tolerate the pain much more. However, if the problem persists, you may want to ease up on the flexion of your foot or focus on the push off of your back foot, which will elongate your muscles.

If stretching still isn't helping your shins, I recommend you try doing what the professionals do. After your walk, go into your shin stretch from the cool-down (see page 99) and then ice your shins: five minutes on, five minutes off. It is also a good idea to regularly massage your shins and to keep stretching them, even if you aren't planning on working out. This will help increase circulation and reduce swelling. Not one of my JayWalkers has ever been forced to stop their journey because of shin problems. But If shin pain becomes a constant problem, then definitely consult with your physician.

and then become contracted. This will help you tone the backs of your legs and your buttocks.

When first trying out Level 1 of JayWalking, you are likely to feel a slight bit of discomfort in your shins. Don't worry about this. With time, and plenty of JayWalking, this will go away. Just keep yourself focused on your breathing, the tightness in your muscles, and the awareness of your underlying emotions. This will keep you in the here and now.

JayWalker: So how do I know when to start and when to finish a certain technique, either mental or physical?

Jay: Trust your instinct. You now have many different techniques from the Mental Journey to help guide you on a wonderful Jay-Walk. You have also been given new ways of focusing on your body physically. Play with them; have fun; make a game out of it. Put your energy into the positive and build a mountain.

There is no right or wrong to JayWalking. You have to remember to do what is most comfortable for you, and what you enjoy.

JayWalker: Are there any positive effects to outdoor exercise?

Jay: Absolutely! Fitness outdoors has the ability to destroy viruses and bacteria associated with illness. Broad Spectrum Sunshine destroys germs and other microorganisms that may linger on your hands or skin. Moderate amounts of UV light also has the tendency to increase calcium absorption in the bones. In other words, Jay-Walking outdoors will decrease the risk of osteoporosis and contribute to a healthier skeletal system. And let's not forget that the trees, plants, and flowers contribute to the environment with carbon dioxide—Mother Nature's natural filter to help purify and clean the air.

Secret to JayWalking Number 1:
Visualization vs. Discomfort

As we learned in the Mental Journey, visualization can be the most powerful tool in manifesting lifelong change. How many of you have begun a workout program or have worked out for a long period of time and stopped because you just couldn't seem to push through to the next level? In this section you will learn how to move beyond that.

Check this out: The University of California at Fresno conducted a study on visualization. They took a group of individuals and connected them to a PET scan (postitron-emission tomography), which measures the activity in the brain, and to an EMG, an electromyograph, which measures the electrical current in an active muscle. While remaining stationary participants were asked to visualize, with emotion, themselves engaging in physical activity, such as running, walking, or riding a bicycle. The amazing thing is that their muscles actually responded to the visualization. Just think: You can achieve physical fitness results without even moving; your body will respond just to visualization. This is one way JayWalking can be done any-time, anywhere.

Now, this doesn't mean that if we apply visualization with emotion to physical exercise, we will become so exhausted that we won't be able to walk, let alone JayWalk. However, you will go to a new level of awareness.

When we begin to exercise, our bodies release repressed emotions such as anger, hostility, anxiety, and confusion. This is when most people throw in the towel. Muscular pain, stiffness, and discomfort are what the physical body creates to avoid our awareness of unpleasant feelings. If you become overwhelmed by physical discomfort, ask yourself, *What am I thinking right now? How am I feeling emotionally, and what could be bothering me?* Observe what's spinning in your tornado of thoughts. The remarkable thing is that if you focus on your emotions rather than the physical discomfort, the brain will pick up on this and you will have a magical relief from pain.

JayWalker: How many days a week do I have to JayWalk to see my body change?

Jay: In order to reap physical fitness benefits, I recommend a forty-five-minute walk three to four days a week. This is a good mainte-nance program which will show visible results and keep you challenged. For permanent weight loss, you have to burn about 1,500 calories a week. Simply put, that's 15–20 miles a week.

JayWalker: How can I rate my performance level and tell whether or not I'm getting stronger, and why is JayWalking better than other impact sports, like running?

Jay: Easy! If you are finishing your usual course in less time and feeling less exhausted, your fitness level is improving. JayWalking is superior to jogging because you reap all, if not more, of the bene-fits of running without the jarring impact. By increasing your walking speed, you'll use more oxygen and burn more calories than when you walk your normal pace. Also, the effect of a runner's daily jostling of the connective tissue wears down the elasticity of the skin. Sagging skin is not what we are looking for in exercising. By JayWalking, you'll look younger longer.

LEVEL 2: JAYWALKING

Now that you have mastered the Stride, it is time to accelerate your walk and use your Mental Journey to JayWalk. With JayWalking your body becomes more challenged and your aesthetic and cardiovascular qualities are greatly increased. In other words, you become a lean, mean, walking machine.

In addition to the benefits of the Stride, JayWalking also offers these fantastic gifts:

Body fat is reduced
Lean muscle mass is increased
Metabolism speeds up
Resting heart rate is lowered (reducing risk of cardiovascular disease)
Bone density is increased
Balance and coordination skills are enhanced

ARM PLACEMENT

In Level 2 of JayWalking, our primary goal is to increase our workload, speed, and fat metabolic rate. In order to do this, we shorten the lever of our arm. Bend the arm from the elbow at a 90-degree angle from the front of your body. Keep the elbow tight to the side of the body, as though you are walking through a narrow alleyway. It's that tight, compact position that will give you more power for your arm swing, increase your shoulder strength and help condition your triceps.

Movement: Begin swinging your arms from the shoulder joints. Be careful to keep your elbows at the ninety-degree angle. Imagine your arms working like the piston on a locomotive train. Move your arm only from the shoulder. Imagine the style a sprinter would take in running a 10-meter dash. Keeping your palms slightly facing the sky will help your elbows stay close to the side of your body. Don't allow your hands to swing past the top of your chest, or to cross over.

A common misconception is that walking is done primarily with the legs. But in order to accelerate calorie burning and cardiovascular benefits, it's all about the arm swing. The arms are what take you from one place to another. The more you punch the elbow behind you, and the more committed you are with the arm swing, the faster your feet will move. Just keep pumping those arms. You'll increase your circulation, burn more calories, and improve your balance.

Walking Technique #2

For an additional free-flowing movement, allow the hips to roll back and forth in a natural swing. Be careful not to overexaggerate this.

FOOT PLACEMENT

Exaggeration is the key. This is very similar to the Stride. Strike the ground with your heel, lifting the toe up toward your knee. Do not overstride. Taking unnaturally long strides will slow you down and greatly reduce your ability to tighten your buttocks and recruit muscle fiber. Allow your foot to roll forward naturally, and push off with your toes.

Movement: Imagine that your knees are wrapped together with a loose, flexible rubber band. You have the ability to stride forward, but if you go too far, your back leg will snap forward, propelling you to the next step. Each and every time you take a step forward, you are striking that heel into the ground, lifting the toe to the knee, and pushing off with the back toes.

I strongly recommend that during your JayWalk you practice a body scan (see the Mental Journey, page 43). Start from the top of your head and work your way down your body. Pay attention to whether or not you are keeping yourself in proper alignment. Imagine that your head is a helium-filled balloon lifting higher to the sky. Is your chin slightly lifted? Are your shoulders directly over your hips? Are your shoulder blades squeezing gently together? Do your abdominals feel lifted and held in? Are you tightening them as you exhale? Don't forget the buttocks—tight, tight, tight.

Another great trick is to imagine that you have ski poles in your hand and that you are in a cross-country ski race. Each time you swing your arm back, you are digging a pole into the snow as you feel that cool, crisp mountain air.

As your speed begins to increase, you will enter the world of Jay-Walking. You'll experience the "high" that most fitness fanatics feel when they work out, often called a runner's high. It's kind of like tapping into your own natural internal drugstore. Tranquility, clarity, relaxation, motivation—all felt by entering the world of JayWalking. You are activating your body's natural ability to heighten awareness of the beauty within you and surrounding you.

By opening your heart and applying the exercises in the Mental Journey, you not only create physical enhancement through power-of-mind techniques, but also emotional enhancement by taking responsibility and just doing. Remember: Don't judge or analyze, just do. *Trying brings doubt. But through doing you make a commitment to yourself and to JayWalking.*

While JayWalking, I don't focus on some sort of an external exercise or technique to give you results. For all of us, in purchasing this program, we are looking for hope and new ideas on our quest to love ourselves more and achieve physical fitness benefits. Remember that somewhere along the line we have lost the true meaning of fitness. As a society we have come to believe that we can find happiness and a more radiant body in a certain fitness program, a fancy technique, a magic pill, or an exercise machine. If that were the case, why haven't we all achieved our fitness dreams already?

Fitness lies within, and it evolves from showing up on a day-to-day basis and finding out what lies beyond the layers of the external shell. This leads to the true essence of who we are and what makes us tick. By applying the exercises in the Mental Journey we begin to have a greater appreciation for ourselves and for the world we live in. It is a much more challenging approach to try and show up on a daily basis and to apply all of these internal techniques than it is to throw the responsibility on some sort of an external focus.

Physical fitness starts at the core of who we are, and gets us to love, accept, and trust our hidden talents. The more comfortable we become with showing up, and with the emotions that are revealed to us, the more physically fit our bodies will become.

QUICK REVIEW OF JAYWALKING

1. Heel strike on the ground (flexing the foot, lifting the toe toward the knee).
2. Rolling through the foot and pressing the toes behind you into the ground.
3. Keep the legs tight together as though your knees were wrapped with a rubber band.
4. Short leg stride, large arm swing.
5. Keep the abs (tummy) held in and lifted.
6. Squeeze the buttocks and slightly roll the hips side to side.
7. Chest lifted.
8. Eyes forward as though driving a car.
9. Arms bent at a 90-degree angle.
10. Palms slightly facing the sky.
11. Incorporate exercises from the Mental Journey.

Secret to JayWalking Number 2:
Isometric Contraction

While you are testing out your new JayWalking stride, it is important to be aware of isometric contraction: muscular contraction without a change in muscle length. Isometric contraction in JayWalking is initiated whenever you tighten your body, either by squeezing in your buttocks, holding in your abdominals, or gently squeezing your shoulder blades back and together. By following this rule and engaging in isometric contraction we recruit more muscle fibers. When we recruit more muscle fibers, the body has to work harder which will assist in burning more calories.

Look at it this way: If you were to walk down the block and squeeze your butt, it would be a bit more difficult than walking down the street relaxed. It's that little bit of applied effort that creates the long-term fitness gain. The real challenge in JayWalking is to maintain isometric contraction throughout the duration of your journey.

You may find it difficult to move smoothly and keep your body isometrically contracted. When I talk about isometric contraction, I'm primarily focusing on your upper back squeeze, the tightness of your buttocks, and the lift of the abdominal wall. *Every other part of the body should be flowing freely.* Keep your arms swinging and legs moving. It would be impossible to keep all of the muscles in your body tightened while creating fluid movement. This is known as a Valsalva maneuver and will raise your blood pressure unnecessarily.

The greatest attribute that isometric contraction has is that it can be performed at any given point in the day, and no one has to know you're doing it. When you get up from your desk to walk to the water fountain—hold in your abs. When you're standing waiting for an elevator at your favorite department store—squeeze your butt. Or when you're walking around the house doing chores—keep your shoulders down and tighten your shoulder blades. Anytime you place a slight bit more stress on your body, your body will begin to respond with physical fitness benefits.

Secret to JayWalking Number 3:
Rate of Perceived Exertion (RPE)

Over the years, fitness experts have come up with many different ways to monitor exercise. However, in JayWalking I have found that monitoring your heart rate is the most effective way to judge whether you are burning fat or just relaxing. In JayWalking, I have made this process as simple as possible. Instead of strapping some fancy apparatus to your body, or adding and subtracting a complex mathematical formula, I'd like you to use my preferred choice of calculation, the rate of perceived exertion (RPE).

In RPE, you are the judge of how you feel, and how you feel will ultimately tell you how hard you are working. Changes in breathing, sweating, heartbeat, and fatigue are your primary indicators for the scale. RPE (based on Borge Scale) is basically a method of comparing your energy level by judging your various activities.

Let's say I asked you to recreate the way you get out of bed in the morning. You would probably have your eyes at half-mast, your coordination would be slightly off, and your vision a bit blurry. Definitely not the way you want to be when you JayWalk. This is probably how you would feel at Level 1 on the RPE scale.

But if we were to turn it around, and I said to you, "Act out the energy level it would take you to catch a bus," you would automatically change the way you carry your body. Your heart rate would increase, your eyes would open wider, and your legs would move faster—definitely a Level 10 on the RPE scale. Get the picture? Energy is all stored in the mind. All we have to do is tap into a memory and reenact the moment. It's our STOP and Super Gluing techniques reenacted.

Latest research shows that RPE is a much more accurate indicator of checking your heart rate than trying to find your pulse on the side of your neck or your wrist. It has been determined that individuals can be up to twenty beats off on a pulse rate check, whereas using the rate of perceived exertion scale, you can assess the situation just by monitoring how you feel.

Below is my RPE chart. You can either use my recommendations or come up with more of your own. Adjust the chart to your specifications and fill in the blanks! Remember the level of energy must relate to the situation.

Level 1. Rolling out of bed
       2. _____
       3. Light housework
       4. _____
       5. Mowing the lawn
       6. _____
       7. Pushing a full grocery cart up a hill
       8. _____
       9. _____
      10. Dashing to catch a runaway bus

You may find that your energy level changes throughout your workout. Invariably the questions asked by most of my clients are of this kind: "Am I burning as many calories at a Level 3 as I am at a Level 7?" I'll tell you what I tell them: You definitely burn more calories at the higher end of the scale than you do at the lower end. However, I suggest you try to stay somewhere in the middle, from 4 to 8. This way your workout will stay more balanced and you won't burn out as quickly.

Now if you don't have a lot of time to spend working out and want to burn a lot of calories, you can with JayWalking. Let's say you only have fifteen minutes to JayWalk. I would recommend you warm up for three minutes or so, and then quickly pick up your pace, maintaining a Level 7 or 8 for the rest of the time. *Shorter periods of time at a higher intensity will give you the same calorie-burning benefit as a thirty-minute workout at Level 2, 3, or 4.* So in actuality you can burn more calories in less time if you JayWalk faster than you will if you JayWalk slower the same distance.

Personally, I don't like to spend a lot of time clocking a mile, for you begin to lose the joy of JayWalking. However, for those of you who are into details, the best way to clock a mile would be to get in your car and drive your favorite route, clocking the mileage on your speedometer. Another would be to go to your local track and ask for a mileage breakdown. Or you can purchase a mileage pedometer. But keep to this simple rule: For every mile walked, approximately one hundred calories are burned.

JayWalker: If JayWalking is a self-esteem enhancer, what is the difference between your program and other self-help books?

Jay: Self-esteem is given to us at birth. It is the most valuable lesson we can learn. Self-esteem cannot be developed simply by reading about it. That doesn't mean that self-help books are not valuable tools. However, with JayWalking, you are given the opportunity to learn through movement and awareness that self-esteem cannot be put on a piece of paper, but must be lived.

Secret to JayWalking Number 4:
Interval Training

Interval training is a fitness technique that will increase your speed and enable you to cover more ground in less time. It also increases the intensity of your workout making you stronger and more energetic, to go that extra mile. By adding short intervals of fast-paced JayWalking to your workout, followed by a recovery period of slow-paced walking, you will not only improve your walk, but you'll also have a more calorie-burning walk on those days when you don't have much time.

Early on in the Mental Journey, I talked about how we can change our physical and emotional state through visualization. Another way to do this is by how we carry ourselves and through our breathing. In interval training, you can create a burst of energy just by changing the way you carry yourself. A great way to experiment with interval training is to find a contained area, such as a large circular drive, a running track, or the border around a large fountain; that way, you'll know your route, and you can really focus on speed and intensity without slowing down. Stay clear of winding roads during this portion of your JayWalk; they will make interval training too difficult.

One advantage of interval training is it can be done at any point in your JayWalk. However, I recommend you wait at least a good ten minutes into your JayWalk, so that your body gets warm enough. That way you won't fatigue too quickly. Sometimes if we create short bursts of energy at the beginning of the JayWalk, our muscles build up lactic acid (that burning, tired feeling), which causes discomfort and fatigue, and prevents us from performing truly effective, exhilarating intervals.

For the most effective results, interval training sets should be performed at a one to three ratio: one minute as fast as you can, followed by three minutes of a slower paced recovery. This is the classic model of interval training.

This doesn't mean that you cannot experiment with other counts and time frames, such as four seconds fast walking, followed by four seconds slower walking. The rule in interval training is to get our bodies to use as much energy as possible in the shortest amount of time. It's that burst of power that is most similar to the power a sprinter would apply to win a race, so the longer you rest between racing spurts the more power you have to give.

In other words, you're training your body to tolerate higher intensities of JayWalking. The whole system of interval training is meant to help you raise your metabolic rate and burn more calories in a faster-paced walk. With enough interval training you will soon find yourself walking at faster levels on the RPE scale.

You may be curious to know what is happening to your body in interval training. During those quick bursts of energy, your lungs are taking in more oxygen, your body is burning more calories, and your heart is being challenged in a healthy way. The heart rate increases, the respiration increases, and the blood pressure increases. In other words, you're mildly stressing your system. It is important in fitness to put a slight amount of stress on the body. This is a key factor in making the body stronger. If we gradually put stress on the body— the heart, the lungs, and the underlying muscle groups—we will increase the rate at which oxygen is moved through it, and in turn, we will increase healthier cellular production and strengthen the heart, which will then be able to hold more blood. The healthier the heart is at rest, the less the heart has to work at rest or play.

The average heart rate for a physically fit person is about 66 to 72 beats per minute. The sedentary person's heart rate could be 80-plus beats per minute. This means that the sedentary person's heart beats approximately 1,200 times more in one hour, not to mention in one day, one month, one year, or a lifetime, than the active person. Please, do yourself a favor. JayWalk and give your heart a rest.

SPEED AND INTENSITY EXERCISE

Now that you've been introduced to interval training, I'd like to take the time to introduce you to a couple sets of exercises that I perform in my classes. Keep in mind with interval training that body alignment and posture are essential. Keep your chin up, shoulders back, chest slightly lifted, abdominals held in, and buttocks tight, and flex your foot by lifting your toe up toward your knee. Imagine your body like an antenna, absorbing all of the energy that surrounds you. I want you to walk for 15 seconds as fast as you can go, followed by 8 seconds at a slower pace. Don't drop your arms, keep your eyes on the road, as though you are driving a car, and let's make it happen. Ready? Set? Go!

15, 14, 13, 12, 11, 10, 9, 8, 7, 6, 5, 4, 3, 2, 1!

Phew! All right! You did it! Breathe deep! Feel the sensations in your body. And keep moving!

Relax and slow down the pace for 8 seconds.

8, 7, 6, 5, 4, 3, 2, 1!

You should now be feeling excellent. Your body is beginning to experience more oxygen uptake and you are probably feeling tired. This technique will increase your metabolism and burn calories more effectively when you're just sitting still.

EXERCISE 2

This time we're going to incorporate our body scanning technique (see the Mental Journey, page 43). We will begin by focusing on the top of the head. Then slowly move your focus from your head and feel the sensations all the way down to your toes. Notice as you scan down your body how each muscle feels, the way your arms swing and the tightness of your buttocks. The body scanning technique will help you to stay focused on the exercise and be in the moment.

Okay, get yourself psyched: This will be an exhilarating experience, one in which you'll really feel the connection of body, mind, and spirit.

Chin lifted, shoulders back, chest high to the sky, abdominals held in and lifted, squeezing the buttocks. All right, let's try it again. Thirty seconds as fast as you can go, focusing on each sensation of your body. On your mark, get set, go!

30. Strike the heel on the ground
29. Feel the stretch behind your heel and calf
28. Go faster
27. Flex that foot
26. Feel your shins—oh, yeah

25. Keep your stride short
24. Breathe
23. Feel the back of your legs
22. Feel the front of your legs
21. Keep it up!
20. Squeeze your butt
19. Awesome
18. Notice the tension in your lower body as opposed to your upper body
17. Fabulous
16. Abdominals lifted
15. Exhale! and hold in your tummy!
14. Energy!
13. Go faster
12. Arms tight to the body
11. Punch those elbows!
10. Feel the stretch in your shoulders as they swing back
9. Neck is long
8. Chin is lifted
7. Breathe!
6. Keep it going
5. Light at the end of the tunnel
4. Breathe!
3. A little faster!
2. Slow it down . . .
1. Relax—

Now drop your arms to the side of your body, slow down your pace, and experience the feelings of exhilaration. It's your day. You deserve it. Just say yes!

Keep in mind that the more you incorporate interval training in your workout, the more energy you'll be able to experience throughout the day. You'll fly up stairs instead of riding an elevator, you'll do three loads of laundry, not one, you'll leap small buildings in a single bound.

I would recommend interval training every time you JayWalk, and even when you're walking in a shopping mall, down the street, or from your car to the grocery store. Fitness is an accumulative effect. Anytime you commit to JayWalking, you create an ideal environment to keep your body motivated, focused, and disciplined to physical fitness—and the benefits are phenomenal.

Below is a list of my favorite interval challenges. Try them out and have some fun.

1. Eight seconds of fast walking followed by four seconds of recovery (slow). Repeat two to ten times in a row.
2. Fifteen seconds of fast walking followed by four seconds of recovery (slow). Don't drop arms. Repeat anytime throughout your workout.
3. Four seconds fast, four seconds slow. Do this for thirty seconds to one minute. This one's challenging.
4. Eight seconds fast, sixteen seconds slow. Good to really increase your power, for your rest period is longer.
5. Fifteen seconds fast, eight seconds slow, eight seconds fast, four seconds slow. Repeat three times.

There is no right or wrong combination with interval training. You can switch these counts around, going JayWalking for five minutes using number 1 and then going right to number 4. Any pattern is correct. Experiment and have fun!

HILLS VS. FLAT SURFACES

Another form of interval training is alternating hills and flat surfaces. Not only is this a great way to exercise, but it adds variety to your JayWalking fitness program. Hills will make your legs stronger and allow you to challenge your heart rate to achieve optimum fitness gains.

Be aware that there is a big difference between going up a hill and going down a hill. Believe it or not, downhill JayWalking is much more challenging. *Downhill walking is more difficult because the acceleration of gravity against the body is quicker than the brain can process.* This causes you to focus on balance and coordination skills, which can slow down your pace. The key to downhill walking is not to focus on speed but to concentrate on your isometric contraction: bending your knees and holding in your abdominals (imagining yourself in a mini-squat position). Keep your arms to your side and swing them at a slower pace.

As you begin to experiment with uphill and downhill walking, you'll notice that as you walk down a hill, your body will slow and so will your heart rate. Downhill walking creates more work for the muscles, enhancing muscle tone in your legs. This process will keep the fat-and calorie-burning level activated. When you go up a hill, I would recommend you focus on your speed, punching those elbows behind you, and keeping the chin lifted. And before I forget, flat surfaces are really the best to increase your speed, for there are no sudden surprises, and you can really go, go, go.

JayWalker: Would the STOP technique and Super Gluing be effective during interval training?

Jay: 110 percent! These two techniques are extremely beneficial in assisting you to push that extra mile. Remember, these are the two techniques that utilize a unique physical movement such as pounding your chest. The physical movement gives me immediate energy and often makes me laugh. Then I really begin to enjoy my interval training. There are also times when I'll play around with my Super Glue technique. I imagine seeing my ideal self with a ball-and-paddle game as I say out loud, "yes, yes, yes!"—pushing myself that extra bit. It's a real blast; you just have to try it.

JayWalker: If the JayWalking program increases self-esteem and motivation, does that mean I will ultimately be happy?

Jay: Improving your self-esteem and motivation level does not guarantee happiness. It does mean that you will have a deeper and more lasting respect for yourself. In other words, loving yourself more, and with more humility, life will still be the same, in the sense that there will still be things out of your control, but you will be able to handle your feelings and your behaviors more graciously. The external stimuli may be the same, but you will look at them much more differently when you have self-esteem and motivation.

CONDITIONING EXERCISES

Once you've mastered your JayWalking technique, it is time to add squats, dips, push-ups, and lunges. All of these are a great way to add more excitement to your walking program and keep you challenged.

When you walk consistently, you experience and feel certain sensations. Your heart races, perspiration begins to increase, you feel your arms swishing against the trunk of your body. But when you stop and perform a series of conditioning exercises, you create a new journey. Your body twitches, quivers, and tingles with excitement. In essence, you wake up a whole new you. The key is to trick the body by consistently varying your JayWalking routine so it doesn't become stagnant, but remains a constant adventure.

The following exercises are designed to complement your Jay-Walking journey. You are probably familiar with some of these from your school days. Others may bring on a new experience. Keep in mind that these exercises should be performed only after you have JayWalked consistently for a good fifteen to twenty minutes; that way you are warmed up and have begun the calorie burning process. Otherwise, you're not giving your body an adequate amount of time to achieve cardiovascular fitness.

For you first-time JayWalkers—or those of you not familiar with cardiovascular or aerobic fitness—I recommend that if you get tired at any time during your JayWalk, you should stop and perform one or two of the following exercises. This will help you catch your breath, as well as keep your heart rate elevated and calories melting away. Do as many repetitions as you can, working your way up to 15–20 reps in one set. *The number of sets plus reps are not important as long as proper alignment and form are emphasized. Increase repetitions as you get stronger.*

UPPER BODY EXERCISES
PUSH-UPS

The ultimate for upper body strength. This exercise will condition your chest, shoulders, and arms. Ideal for those of you who are looking for a little enhancement in the chest area.

Position: A park bench, large tree, or the side of a car are all great places to perform this movement. Place hands slightly wider than your shoulders, leaning your body forward, feet together, knees slightly soft, squeezing your buttocks and holding in your abdominals. Your body should be at a 45 degree angle from the ground. Keep chin lifted, don't look down.

Push-Ups—Position 1

Push-Ups—Position 2

Movement: Bend elbows slightly out to the side, lowering your chest to about three inches from the bench. *Inhale when bending elbows on the way down, exhale when pushing up.* The body doesn't bend when doing push-ups. Keep your body in alignment like a board from head to toe.

Journey: On the downward phase of the movement, focus on the stretch you are feeling from the side of your chest to under your arms. As you exhale, imagine you are squeezing your chest together, keeping it tight and tense. Imagine your arms meeting one another in the upward phase of the movement.

This exercise instills confidence, supports the diaphragm, which is beneficial to proper breathing, and helps clear congestion.

TRICEPS DIPS

Excellent for the back of the upper arm. If you're self-conscious about this area of your body, this exercise will create tone and enhancement to keep you free from those jiggling underarms.

Position: Sitting up straight on a park bench, wall, or fence, place your hands down to the side of your hips, a little wider than

Triceps Dips—Position 1

Triceps Dips—Position 2

your shoulders. Make sure fingertips are facing forward. Keep chin lifted, shoulders back, and chest high to the sky. Again, hold abdominals in, to stabilize the body.

Movement: Keep elbows facing directly behind you; avoid letting them open to the side. Slowly bend elbows, supporting your body weight, exhaling up. Inhale down and straighten your arms on the way up without locking your elbows. Make sure you are keeping your chin lifted and bending your elbows.

Journey: Notice the sensation of stretching in the back of your arms as you bend your elbows. Be aware of the challenge at each phase of the movement. *As you exhale up, focus on tightening the back of your arms without snapping your elbow.*

By doing this exercise you are working muscles you may rarely use. This exercise represents the capacity to participate in the joys of life, accept new experiences, and forgive past indiscretions.

ABDOMINALS

Now I'd like to talk briefly about your tummy, the abdominal area. Most of us are looking for a firmer, flatter tummy. When doing your abdominal exercises, keep in mind that your entire midsection is included in this. It is the muscle group that runs from below your chest all the day down past your belly button. It is responsible for supporting your back, as well as your postural alignment. Training and toning this muscle group can be the most difficult of all.

The great thing about JayWalking is that at any given point in the day, you can tighten your tummy. When you JayWalk, you increase your heart rate, and you begin burning more body fat, the cushion-like layers around your midsection. As the body fat decreases, the abdominal definition and sculpting effects will begin to show. So all you need to do is show up, apply the knowledge, walk in proper form and your body will blossom. Adding the following exercises will only enhance the definition and help give you the tummy you've always dreamed of. So get ready gang, and tuck!

STANDING ABDOMINAL CRUNCHES

The best thing about this exercise is that you can sculpt your abs and no one ever has to know you're doing it.

Position: Standing upright with knees slightly bent, gently tilt the buttocks and pelvis forward under your body. Place your hands on your waist, behind your head, or alongside your body.

Movement: Exhale, scoop out your abs in a concave fashion and with small movements, lean the trunk forward. Keeping a slight tension on the abs, *inhale on the way up and exhale on the way down.*

Standing Abdominal Crunches

Journey: As you exhale, imagine that the bottom of your rib cage is being pushed against your pelvis. Your belly button is sinking deeper and deeper through your body into your lower back. Visualize your abdominals becoming sculpted, tight, toned, and enhanced.

ABDOMINAL KNEE-UPS

This is an excellent exercise—you get to sit down for a minute—to tone the abdominal area and stretch the lower back.

Position: Sit on a park bench and lean back. Slide your buttocks as far forward as possible. Place your hands on the bench, slightly wider than your shoulders and to the sides of your hips, and grip the edge of the bench. Tilt your pelvis forward and slightly round your back.

It is important here to protect your lower back by concaving your body, scooping out your tummy. Imagine you are sinking your belly button through your body into your lower back.

Movement: Slowly raise your knees toward your shoulders and chest. Imagine that you are sinking your belly button into your lower

Abdominal Knee-Ups

back. Do not be con-
cerned if you cannot get
your knees all the way up
toward your shoulders.
This movement comes
from the hip joint (*if you
feel discomfort in the
lower back, place one foot
on the ground and focus
on lifting one knee at a
time*).

Journey: Focus on
keeping your pelvis tucked under. Notice the sensations you feel in
your tummy. How does the top of the tummy feel, as opposed to the
belly button? What does it feel like when the legs are lower as
opposed to higher? Challenge yourself by keeping the tension away
from the handgrip and in the abdominals. Breathing is the key:
exhaling on the way up, inhaling on the way down.

Abdominals represent the digestion of thoughts and ideas. They
are the body's stored resource for energy.

REVERSE ABDOMINAL CRUNCHES

This exercise can only be performed on a park bench that has a
back. It's excellent for you beginners
and those of you who want to add
variety to your abdominal routine.

Position: Siting backward on a
park bench, lock your knees under
the back of the bench for support and
set your feet about a foot apart. Place
your fingertips against the side of
your head, elbows open to side.

Movement: Slowly lower your
body back, until you begin to feel ten-

Reverse Abdominal Crunches

sion in your abdominal wall. *Be careful not to lean too far back. Inhale on the way down, exhale on the way up, keeping the pelvis slightly under your body.* Scoop out your tummy. You may want to squeeze your butt cheeks slightly for more control.

Journey: Imagine your body is being scooped out from below your chest to below your belly button. Every time you exhale on the way up, think of your tummy getting flatter, your belly button sinking in more, until it feels as though it is pushing into the lower back. Notice the stretching sensation in your lower back during the upward phase of the movement. This is a great way to ease tension of the back as well as to tone the abdominal region.

LOWER BODY EXERCISES

Firm thighs, sculpted calves, and a perky butt are all achieved by applying the following exercises.

SQUATS

I love to include this exercise in my JayWalking class whenever we stumble upon a busy intersection or after a vigorous climb up a steep hill. By performing this movement, slow or fast, in repetitive fashion, you will keep your heart rate sustained and sculpt your lower body for more strength and agility. It's unbeatable for toning the buttocks and the front of the legs, as well as the back of the legs.

Position: Stand upright with your feet about hip-width apart, toes slightly pointed outward, chin lifted, shoulders back, chest open. Looking straight ahead, place your hands on your hips. Keep your knees slightly bent.

Movement: Bend your knees and point your buttocks directly behind

Squats #1

Squats #2

you, as if you're sitting in a chair, watch to be sure you keep your knees over the center of your foot. Try and keep your chin and chest lifted, with the shoulders slightly behind your ears. Keep your body weight over your heels and avoid leaning the upper body too far forward. The top of your head should be facing the sky, with arms reaching forward, do not lower the buttocks beyond knee level. Then rise back up and repeat.

Journey: Whenever I do this exercise, I feel as if I'm skiing in a James Bond movie. I'm on the top of a mountain in the Swiss Alps. My mission is to get to the bottom of the mountain before the enemy catches up with me. I feel the icy chill of wind against my face. I watch the sun's rays reflect across the landscape, and I dig those poles faster and faster into the snow as I plummet down the hill, feeling every bit of my lower body working harder and harder. I can feel the front, back, and sides of my legs fatiguing, up and down I go, feeling as though I can't go on, but I know what lies behind me and the freedom that lies in front of me. Go for the burn!

LUNGES

Sitting down will not be your favorite leisure activity the day after performing this exercise, but lunges will definitely define your lower half, lifting your derriere and adding sculpture to the front and back of your legs. Oh, come on, don't be scared.

Position: A step or a curb is the best place to perform this movement. Keep your hands on your waist, chin slightly lifted, shoulders back, abdominals supported, and separate your feet about 6 to 12 inches. Keep knees soft and unlocked. Take a step or two back away from the step or curb.

Movement: Lunge forward and place one foot on the step, try to

Lunges

keep the front knee over the center of your foot. This will keep you aligned and give you more stability. Push away, and as you return, bring your foot back and stand in an upright position. Try the movement a few times. Your back knee should be bent slightly and facing the ground. Lift your back heel slightly and keep your pelvis tucked lightly under your body. *Exhaling up and inhaling down.* Repeat using the opposite leg 5–20 times.

Journey: I like to play a game with myself: *I alternate squeezing my right butt cheek when my left foot is forward and squeezing my left butt cheek when my right foot is forward.* I work on keeping a smooth rhythm with this movement while continuing to focus on my butt and the front and back of my leg. Feel those sensations and sculpt that body away.

This movement represents our understanding for ourselves, of life, and of others. It also gives us the ability to be more grounded.

WALKING LUNGES

Very similar to the lunge, without a step for support, this exercise will increase your balance and dexterity as a stationary lunge does, but also keep you moving. It's extremely challenging after a trip to the top of a hill.

Position: Start in an upright position. Again, keep shoulders back, chest lifted, and abdominals in. Don't look down or you will lose your balance. Keep your body weight over your toes and hands on waist.

Movement: Take a large step for-

Walking Lunges

ward. Emphasis: Push your front heel into the ground. Bend your knee and drop your back knee as close to the ground as possible. Immediately pick up your back foot, standing up and bringing your leg forward, alternating sides. Stay low to the ground and keep on lunging. Maintain front knee over center of foot and keep up body lifted. *Exhale up and inhale down.*

Journey: Because this movement is advanced and challenging, I like to help keep myself lighter on my feet and focused by imagining my head is a helium-filled balloon which is lifting my body parts one after the other to the sky. You can also try to find a location in the distance and focus on it to help you keep your balance. Go on a mental journey and create something magical in that place.

ABDUCTION SQUATS

You say saddlebags, do you? Not anymore. With consistent repetition on this movement, you can reshape your outer thighs, buttocks, and the front and back of your legs. That way, you can keep the saddlebag where it belongs—on the horse.

Position: Look straight keeping your chin slightly lifted, shoulders slightly back, abdominals held in, and place yourself in a semi-squat position, hands crossed in front of chest, elbows pointing out to the side.

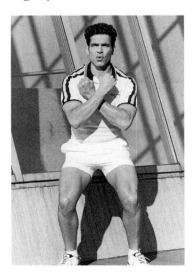

Abduction Squats #1

Movement: Stand up and reach your arms directly over your head, reaching for the sky. Simultaneously extend your right leg straight out to the side, keeping your foot flexed. Keep your standing leg slightly bent, *pause,* bring right leg back to ground and extend left leg. Alternate sides, focusing on side of butt. *Exhale up and inhale down.*

Journey: Notice what your arms are doing here. Don't let momentum take over. Keep your arms strong. I like to think about reaching my fingertips to the sky, but keeping my shoulders down. That way I really feel the work in my arms. Imagine you are one of those pull-string dolls, and when you pull down on the string the arms and the legs of the doll extend out and up. Challenge yourself by trying to keep your leg as straight as possible when you lift it out to the side. What does this exercise remind you of? See it, act it, create it.

This exercise can help you to carry your body in perfect balance. It creates momentum in moving forward through life.

Abduction Squats #2

KICKBACKS

If your lower back is a weak area, and your buttocks needs lifting, this exercise is for you. Keep in mind you should not feel any discomfort in your lower back. Think of keeping your lower back quiet, but putting tension in the buttocks.

Kickbacks

Position: Standing upright with your feet shoulder-width apart and your chin lifted, push your shoulders back, hold your abdominals in, and hold your arms in front of you. Bend your knees slightly and tighten your buttocks.

Movement: Place body into a semisquat position; stand up and reach your arms over your head to the sky. Kick your right leg back and focus on squeezing your right butt cheek. Go back into a squat and alternate sides.

Journey: When kicking your leg behind you, *squeeze the buttocks not the lower back*. Open your chest to the sky and imagine that you are scooping energy into your body every time you bring the arms down. Experience the stretch in your abdominal wall when you reach your fingertips to the sky. Feel the stresses of life escape from you on each and every repetition. Energy, focus, enthusiasm, life!

This movement represents power and strength, and helps release anger.

ARM DRILLS

If your legs get tired and you're determined to burn fat, here's an exercise that will come in handy. This movement will train and strengthen your shoulders, chest, back, and triceps, so your JayWalk will have more power. Think of it as an interval training exercise for your upper body. It's excellent if you have upper back tension; the movement will help release your stress.

I like to do this one on a large staircase because I find that the position of my body keeps me more stabilized. However, it can be performed going up a hill or on a flat terrain.

Position: Go to a set of stairs and place one leg on a higher step and the other on a lower step. Bend the knees and keep bodyweight slightly forward, chin lifted, shoulders back, and arms at a 90-degree angle.

Movement: Punch, strike, and jab your elbows behind you. Don't allow your hands to fly over your shoulders. *Keep your lower body and abdominals isometrically contracted (tightened)*. Work this movement on an 8-second count, and then move one step forward, and repeat. Example: Swing arms aggressively—8, 7, 6, 5, 4, 3, 2, and 1. Take a step. Again: 8, 7, 6, arms faster, 5, 4, 3, 2, 1.

Journey: Have you ever had a dream where you are being chased and felt as if you were running and running and running but not getting anywhere? This journey takes you back to that place. What is behind you is defeat, and what is in front of you is your destiny. Commit to that arm swing and watch where that destiny can take you.

STAIR CLIMBING

Stair climbing will enhance the firmness of your buttocks, break up the monotony of even, level terrain, and help stabilize your knees by strengthening your quadriceps.

Position: Keep your eyes looking up at the top of the staircase, chin up. Your arms can maintain their JayWalking position, bent at a 90-degree angle, or you can drop your arms to your side for less of a challenge. Place one foot forward and one foot back, knees slightly bent.

Movement: Holding in your abs, place one foot in front of the other and go. Try taking two steps at a time for an added challenge. Remember to keep your knees facing forward. Think of pressing your heel, not your toe, into each step you take. This way you accentuate the contraction in your buttocks.

Journey: For each step I take, I reflect upon my accomplishments in life, large and small. From my career and financial gains, to the small extension of opening a door for a needy person. With each and every step, I bring to my body the power to face any obstacles that may come my way and to climb the stairway to success. Remember: We don't know where we're going unless we know where we've been.

QUADRICEPS EXTENSIONS

A large core of my JayWalking group were originally aggressive runners. After many years of wear and tear on the knees, walking has now become their sport of choice. Because the knee joint doesn't consist of any muscle to keep it strong and stabilized, the next best thing is to strengthen the areas around it. This way, a support system is instilled, an internal muscular brace that reduces discomfort and frees mobility.

Position: Sitting on a bench or chair, keep your chin slightly lifted and open up your chest by keeping your shoulders back. Hands should be placed shoulder-width apart behind hips, with fingertips facing the back. This way, you can prop your body up, keeping yourself tall and lifted.

Movement: Keep your left foot on the ground and extend right leg straight out, keeping knee straight. Hold in air for a second and return right foot to ground. Repeat ten to twenty times and switch to other leg. *Exhale up, and inhale down.*

Try to keep lifting the leg as straight as possible, and avoid sinking your chest.

Journey: Your heel has a thread attached to it. As you lift your working leg, imagine you have your own personal fitness coach and he is pulling the string away from you. Who is this person? What does he or she look like? How does this person make you feel? What does this bring to your exercise? As the string is being pulled, feel the tightness in your quadriceps. Don't ignore the sensation, but focus on it. Try and keep your abdominals as strong and tight as possible. Stay confident that you can get through it. This exercise can be done many times on each leg. Remember: Who is your imaginary fitness coach? And what does he or she bring to your workout?

The quadriceps represents repressed strains and tension. This movement stimulates circulation, which helps clear the body of toxins.

JayWalker: Could positive affirmations be effective during conditioning exercises?

Jay: Yes. Every technique discussed in the Mental Journey can be applied to the Physical Journey. Again, the great thing about Jay-Walking is that there is no wrong; everything is right. If you forget a movement or a thought, you'll always have something to draw upon. I like to use my positive affirmations during the conditioning exercises because it really gets me into the moment. For example, if I say something positive during a push-up, such as I'm strong, I'm confident, I'm amazing, *it'll give me that extra edge to get through those last couple of repetitions. Give it a shot. You'll see what I mean.*

JayWalker: How will JayWalking get me in touch with my feelings?

Jay: JayWalking is the ultimate fitness journey. In any physical fitness journey, our bodies become dilated, open, and receptive. The veins, arteries, and capillaries of the body enable the blood to flow more freely. In essence, the same is happening with the mind and the emotions. When we JayWalk, oxygen uptake is increased; therefore, there is more oxygen going to the brain cells, creating a clearer, more open and receptive thought process. This enables you to feel more clearly. Accept your feelings without fear. Don't be afraid of your humanness. Embrace it and you will no longer fear your emotions.

COOL-DOWN

Way to go! You made it!

Take a moment to slow down and begin to feel how energized and alive your body feels. It's now time to truly reap the rewards of a job well done. The cool-down is designed to bring your pulse rate back to a more comfortable resting state. It allows your cardiovascular system to gently slow down, and brings your body temperature to a cooler level. It is important to remember that when we initiate our cool-down, it is a gradual process. Slowly lower your pace to a comfortable stroll and allow your arms to drop to the side of your body. This way, your body gets a chance to adjust. I don't recommend stopping abruptly after you JayWalk. In other words, don't walk for fifteen to forty minutes and then have a seat on a park bench. Take the time to slow down. Enjoy the sensations from work well done. Notice your body tingle. Notice the glow in your skin. Notice the elated rise in your awareness. It's a good idea to cool down for two to five minutes before coming to a complete stop.

FINAL STRETCHING

I don't have time. I'm running late. How often do we hear this one? Many of my clients love to JayWalk, but when it comes time for the final stretching at the end of a class, forget about it, they're on their way to the next appointment. Little do they know that the next appointment could be with their doctor. The final stretch is extremely important to help elongate your muscles after a JayWalk, which will help them recover faster, so that you will have less chance of developing soreness and cramping later on. *In addition, final stretching helps improve your overall flexibility. So not only will you achieve fat-burning and toning benefits, but you'll be able to touch your toes again, and maybe even lift your legs over your head!*

The stretches in the cool-down section of your JayWalk are very similar to your warm-up stretches at the beginning. The only difference here is that you hold your stretches for a good fifteen to thirty seconds, no bouncing, no moving. This is what is called a static stretch. The static stretch is designed so that your body can begin its relaxation process. You may notice a bit more flexibility at the end of a JayWalk, due to the fact that your body has become well warmed, for only warm muscles can be stretched effectively. *If you stretch three to five days a week, you will increase flexibility, and two to three days a week will maintain flexibility.* So utilize this time to create that youthful mobility.

At the beginning of our journey, we started out stretching from the ground up, bringing in the energy from the earth to our bodies. In clos-ing, let's collect all of the energy that we experienced on our journey—such as the cloud formations, the colors, the shapes, any people we may have passed, the feeling of the air, the sounds, the trees, any life form that could have brought awareness to our day—and begin to acknowledge its presence, absorbing the energy from the top of our head to our toes. Follow me now as we close our Physical Journey.

Neck Stretch

NECK STRETCH

Stand in an upright position, feet shoulder-width apart, knees slightly bent, shoulders back and relaxed, and pelvis neutral. Place one hand at the small of your lower back, and the other hand over the top of your head, and pull your head to your shoulder with gentle pressure. Hold fifteen to thirty seconds, feeling the stretch on the opposite side of the neck and upper back. Alternate sides. (This stretch can also be done by placing both hands behind the head and feeling the stretch in the back of the neck.)

Shoulder Stretch

SHOULDER STRETCH

Standing in an upright position, feet shoulder-width apart and knees slightly bent, cross a straightened arm over your chest, place your other hand above the elbow and push toward chest. Imagine reaching your fingertips away from your body. Keep your shoulders relaxed and neck long.

BACK STRETCH 1

Standing in an upright position, feet about shoulder-width apart, interlock your fingers and tilt the pelvis slightly forward, scooping out your abs and keeping your knees bent. Reach both arms over the right side of your body, feeling stretch along the left side of your back. *Hold fifteen to thirty seconds. Repeat to other side.*

Back Stretch #1

BACK STRETCH 2

I recommend this one if you have a park bench handy. Separate your feet, slightly wider than shoulder-width, and place your hands at the top back of the bench. Stretch your buttocks directly behind you, imagining that your tailbone is reaching away. To enhance this stretch, bend your knees, moving into a squat position, and slowly place your hands at lower back of bench. Take your time on this one. You'll love it.

HAMSTRING STRETCH 1

This is similar to the warm-up stretch with-

Back Stretch #2

Hamstring Stretch #1   *Hamstring Stretch #2*

out movement. Start in an upright position, lean your body slightly into left hip, supporting your weight above the left knee. Extend your right leg, flexing foot. Slowly lean body forward, reach toward the foot, pulling your toe toward your knee. *Imagine lifting your buttocks up toward the sky, increasing tension behind your right leg.* Stay with this stretch a little longer, and your hamstrings will thank you later. If you can't reach your foot just lean forward and place both hands above left knee. Hold.

HAMSTRING STRETCH 2

Cross your left leg in front of your right leg. Lean forward and touch the ground. Try to keep back extended to feel the stretch. Hold for thirty seconds and alternate sides. Roll body up slowly.

QUADRICEPS STRETCH 1

This is similar to the warm-up stretch. Standing with your feet shoulder-width apart, upper body lifted, place right foot on a bench or curb. Slide left leg slowly behind and press pelvis forward and hold for fifteen to thirty seconds.

QUADRICEPS STRETCH 2

This stretch will also help with your balance. Keeping the upper body tall, shoulders slightly back, chest lifted, and chin up, pull your left foot up behind you and grasp with left hand. Raise heel as high as possible up to your buttocks and tilt pelvis forward. Hold for thirty seconds. Alternate legs.

Quadriceps Stretch #2

SHIN STRETCH

You'll thank yourself for stretching your shins at the conclusion of a beautiful JayWalk. Stand tall and cross one leg over the other so the back of one calf is against the opposite shin. *Point your front foot into the ground. Press your back knee in back of front leg your legs are slightly bent at this point.* Do you feel a stretching sensation now? Good! Keep it up for a few seconds. If you don't feel a stretch, roll your front foot forward more, and push forward on the leg from behind your calf to stretch it from the ankle to the knee. Really feel it. Switch legs and repeat. *Ahhh!*

Shin Stretch

JayWalker: During my cool-down, I find it very effective to perform a body scan. Is this recommended?

Jay: Trust yourself. It all works. Body scanning will get you in touch with your physical self. Positive affirmations keep you assured, visualizations increase your commitment, STOP and Super Gluing motivate you and give you immediate energy. Do them all, have a ball, and create a new and exciting journey every time you JayWalk.

JayWalker: Will JayWalking give me more self-control?

Jay: The problem with control is that our Western philosophy trains us that power and manipulation are valuable things. But, you see, the problem is that that is an illusion. The only thing in our control is the way we choose to feel about ourselves and the behaviors we choose to express. There is nothing else within our control. As long as we adopt the illusion of control and feel as though we're responsible for things that are not in our control, we cannot live realistic lives and gain the mastery of ourselves.

I hope the Physical Journey of your JayWalking was as exciting and fulfilling for you as it was for me. I'd like you to join me now in finishing up your fitness walk with a closing gesture. *Keeping your feet together, come up on your tippy toes as high as you can, reach your fingertips to the sky, and accept what is rightfully yours for a job well done. You deserve it! Stretch higher and higher, feeling the energy from the sky awaken all of your hidden talents. Express yourself. Be humble. Be alive, and share all of your wonderful gifts.*

And join me again for our next journey in JayWalking.

EXERCISE MODIFICATIONS

Obesity, heart disease, arthritis, and diabetes. These are just a few of the many medical disorders that affect more than 60 percent of our population. The good news is that with a regimen of proper exercise and diet, many of these symptoms can be reduced by up to 70 percent. Imagine that. *Keep in mind that success is a choice, not a change. You have to make the decision to be fit. Don't just wait for your ship to come in. Swim out to get it.* You'll be glad you did. The Jay-Walking program is the ultimate fitness journey for those people worried that too much exercise might not be good for them. With JayWalking you can start with small steps and work at your own pace. Do not let your physical problems discourage you. Look at them as a gift that is enabling you to explore the deeper facets of who you truly are. Make sure you get approval from your physician before starting to JayWalk.

CARDIOVASCULAR DISORDERS

People with hypertension, coronary artery disease, and arteriosclerosis constitute the largest population of exercisers with specific health challenges. Such individuals should focus on a longer warm-up and cool-down. Isometric contraction should be avoided (this may intensify the heart rate and increase blood pressure). Medications, such as beta-blockers, have a tendency to lower the heart rate. Therefore, you may think you are not working hard enough. Use the RPE test (page 70) to assess your workload. Focus on exercises from the Mental Journey: breathing, Super Gluing, visualization, and stress management techniques. Add lots of conditioning exercises to your workout (push-ups, squats, dips), and work up to 30 or 40 minutes of exercise three to four times a week.

RESPIRATORY DISORDERS

Although breathing is a key component to cardiovascular exercise, individuals with chronic respiratory problems can greatly increase their aerobic effectiveness just by applying visualization techniques (see the Mental Journey).

Asthma

Eighty percent of asthmatics experience attacks during exercise. These can be controlled by bronchodilators and medications to assist in breathing. The medications are especially useful during exercise. Sometimes asthmatics will induce an asthma attack before exercise, because by inducing an attack, they make it unlikely that they will experience another attack in the next 30 minutes. A gradual warm-up and cool-down is strongly suggested to prevent overexertion of the respiratory system. Avoid highly polluted areas, extreme temperatures, and days of high pollen count, as these can affect breathing. Cold air can also induce asthma attacks. Be cautious in the winter months, and cover your mouth with a scarf or mask. JayWalking in intermittent segments throughout the day, such as two 15-minute sessions will greatly reduce the risk of attacks. Keep in mind that with consistent focus on visualizations and breathing techniques, improvements can be achieved. JayWalk four to five times per week and be in the here and now.

Bronchitis/Emphysema

JayWalking is extremely successful in relieving chronic, obstructive pulmonary diseases. Aerobic benefits may be limited due to lack of oxygen intake, but they are still possible. Individuals can experience reduced anxiety, lower body weight, more positive thought patterns, and improvement in normal daily functions simply by being in the here and now. (Gee, I wonder if a positive mental attitude has something to do with the results.) JayWalk at least ten minutes in total, but don't exceed 40 minutes. *Avoid upper body arm swing, for this places undue stress on the respiratory system.* Warm up slowly, for at least 10 minutes. Work out three to four times per week.

ORTHOPEDIC DISORDERS

Medical experts refer to back and knee pain as the most expensive benign health condition in America. Thirty-five percent of all workmen's compensation claims are for these disorders and pay out more than ten billion dollars annually. I would strongly suggest that you read Dr. John Sarno's book *Healing Back Pain*. It may challenge your body and your thoughts; however, it could also be your ticket to pain-free living. Keep in mind that JayWalking will increase your range of motion, and therefore you will have more flexibility in your daily functions.

ARTHRITIS

JayWalking will greatly improve your underlying musculature, which will assist in proper joint mobility. *The surgeon general's report says that 30 minutes of exercise a day, done in five-minute intervals, is a great way for arthritics to achieve physical fitness benefits.* Pay special attention to form and posture (shoulders back, chest lifted, chin up). If conditioning exercises are too difficult, focus on isometric contraction (squeeze butt, hold tummy in, keep body tight). This will create wonderful sculpting effects and keep your body stabilized. Focus on mental and spiritual elements.

METABOLIC DISORDERS

Diabetes type I and type II, hypo- and hyperglycemia—all are affected tremendously by dietary food choices. *Eating six small meals a day will keep blood sugar levels balanced, creating sustained energy for an effective exercise program.* The JayWalking fitness journey is extremely beneficial for individuals with metabolic disorders. Body-scanning techniques, breathing exercises, and visualization have been shown to be extremely effective in correcting hormonal imbalances in the system. For those of you Type I insulin-dependent diabetics out there, I recommend insulin injections be avoided in your shoulders and lower body during your JayWalk, for active muscles absorb insulin much too quickly. I recommend that you have a sports bar or a package of sports gel or, better yet, glucose tablets on hand. These products contain high levels of glucose, which is readily absorbed into the system, and they are easy to carry on your JayWalk. Gradually increase your workout to 4 to 5 times a week.

PREGNANCY

Rock a bye baby on the tree top. How many times have we heard this ever-popular song lyric? Probably as many times as we've heard the following excuses during pregnancy: *My body is just not the same since I've had Junior,* or *Once you have a baby, forget it—your youthful figure is gone,* or *Oh, my aching back.* Those are such great excuses not to show up and JayWalk, but I must tell you I have witnessed just as many stories of women who have become more physically fit after pregnancy than they were before. All because they partook of an exercise program during pregnancy. For most women, pregnancy is the perfect time to kick back and relax: Eat all you want, act upon those immediate cravings, such as pickles and ice cream, and indulge in those fatty desserts. After all, that's what's supposed to happen, isn't it? Or so they say. And then, if you're really lucky, you may even get catered to by your husband or your best friend, who will take care of those hard-to-manage odds and ends as you continue to spread wider and wider on the couch. Look: I'm not saying that your energy level is going to be spectacular—especially during your first and last trimester—or that exercise is going to rate number one on your Top 10 list, but I will tell you this: You have received such a wonderful opportunity to acknowledge the life within you, and what better way to express it than by JayWalking? Not only is your baby going to be a gift to the world, but your baby can also help to motivate you to begin an exercise program. *If not for you, what about for him or her?*

Walking is the number one choice of exercise for pregnant women. Not only does it take no special skill, but it will help develop balance and stability while carrying, and also give you a closer bond with the child within. Most of my clients who have been pregnant during their walking program said their unborn baby was happier while they were JayWalking. One woman told me she felt as though the unborn baby would dance around whenever she began JayWalking. Another told me that every morning before she would step outdoors to JayWalk, her baby would kick her, giving her the message to get a move on.

During this new and fulfilling journey, I recommend you keep yourself well hydrated, lay off intense interval training, and pay close attention to what your body is telling you throughout your walk. *The best way to play it safe is to keep checking back with your RPE chart, staying at the lower level, around 4 or 5, and remember, if you can't carry on a conversation while walking, you're not playing it safe.*

Incorporating conditioning exercises into your JayWalk during pregnancy is a wonderful way to not only catch your breath but keep your underlying muscle groups toned and tight. I also recommend Kegell's exercises. In these you tighten the pelvic muscles, as if you are waiting on line for the bathroom. Always remember that during pregnancy your body creates a chemical called relaxin. This chemical makes the joints of your body much more flexible, which can make you more prone to injury. So watch your ankles and knees. By JayWalking, you train your body to maintain isometric contraction, which helps strengthen your underlying muscle groups, so you have less chance of injury and more chance to spring back to your old self after delivery.

Don't get discouraged. Do what you can. If this is your first attempt with an exercise program, consult with your doctor for the clearance and then start out slow, take in the fresh air.

JayWalking is an excellent addition to your fitness program. Not only are you in complete control of your workout—in other words, you have the option of going up a hill or staying on a flat surface, interval training or conditioning exercises—but with walking you can train your overall body with minimal stress and achieve maximum fitness benefits. I wouldn't recommend increasing your fitness level during pregnancy, but it sure is a wonderful opportunity to maintain your health so you can fit back into those favorite jeans. Remember the key is, do what you can. Don't elevate your body temperature too rapidly, and if bleeding or spotting occurs, get thee to a doctor. Remember, exercise can have a wonderfully positive effect on your life, especially during pregnancy. It can

Create new awareness of body
Create greater circulation/less chance of swollen ankles
Encourage a more comfortable delivery
Improve balance and coordination
Enhance cardiovascular fitness and endurance
Provide more energy throughout the day
Prevent varicose veins and blood clotting
Bring on a sense of well-being and balanced emotions
Lead to a quicker recovery to prepregnancy weight(!)

Although walking is the safest exercise for you and your unborn baby, it is still a good idea for you to consult with your doctor, especially if you have a history of miscarrying, premature dilation, multiple pregnancies, or other complications. Avoid jarring activities that produce a high heart rate, or fast and aggressive movements. Be cautious not to overstress muscles and joints.

FOOD IS FUEL

Since all the fitness books on the shelves do it, I'd have to be a fool not to include a brief chapter on nutrition. Although JayWalking is a philosophy, one cannot achieve peak performance in it without the proper diet.

Nutrition and exercise complement one another, kind of like a toothbrush and toothpaste: You can't use one without the other and expect to get the same results. It seems that people will try any new and exciting diet fad, from magic pills, to quick-loss shakes, to cottage cheese and grapefruit. The question I ask myself over and over again is, *Why do we resort to these external remedies to assist our obsession to be thin when we know that fitness is found within?* Plain and simple, because they take little or no effort. Wash a pill down with some water, drink a shake for lunch, have a grapefruit with a cup of coffee—these are all easy. So how about getting up in the morning, rain or shine, and going for a little JayWalk? *Ahhh!* Completely different response, eh? Maybe that's why the diet industry cranks in approximately 25 billion dollars a year and the fitness industry only about 8.5 billion.

Not only are these diets worthless, they are also not nutritional. Without proper nutritional guidance, dieting can place a great deal of stress on your system. For example: A minimal iron deficiency results in reduced oxygen to the tissues of the brain, which can leave you feeling tired, irritable, and unfocused. Also, an inadequate intake of B vitamins stresses the ability of your cells to convert carbohydrates and fat into energy. Too little beta-carotene, vitamins C and E, and selenium weaken the body's antioxidant defenses, which makes the tissues of your body susceptible to stress, damage, and disease. When we become stressed, we are even more vulnerable to nutritional deficiencies. This includes any kind of stress: mental stress at work, the loss of a loved one, the physical stress of an injury to the body, or a surgical procedure. Even environmental stress, such as loud obnoxious sounds, severe weather conditions, and highly polluted air—all upset the nutritional balance. Mental, emotional, and environmental stress can suppress the immune system, resulting in colds, infections, and disease. *That is why I recommend proper nutritional choices. For if the stresses are all short-lived, and you are well-nourished, your body will combat the effect and cope more efficiently.*

Good nutrition doesn't have to be a complicated, drawn-out process. It can be as simple as consuming six to eight ounces of lean protein a day (three ounces is about the size of a deck of cards or the palm of a hand, equivalent to two chicken breasts, five egg whites, or three cups of nonfat yogurt). Eat lots of fruits and vegetables, five to six servings a day. Consume mostly whole-grain products, such as wheat, barley, rye, couscous, kasha, or quinoa. Avoid heavy, greasy foods, and drink plenty of water, the breakfast of champions.

Another way to look at good nutrition is by looking at nature. The strongest, most powerful animals in the world are herbivores. This means that these animals consume only large amounts of vegetation and plant life. Could this be why they live so much longer than carnivorous, meat-eating animals? Herbivores seem to have more energy, are less susceptible to disease, and have longer life spans.

Now, I'm not saying that you have to become a vegetarian, but vegetables and fruits should be the foundation of your daily diet. Americans on average consume only about a third of the amount of fruits and vegetables recommended to give their bodies proper nutrients. This creates many health problems, including digestive, metabolic, and skin disorders, and lack of physical strength and energy.

An easy way to catch up on those fruits and vegetables is by drinking more juice. *Fresh-squeezed juice contains 70 percent more nutrients than over-the-counter packaged juices.* In order to get all of the vitamins and nutrients necessary, we would have to consume fifteen pounds of raw vegetables and fruits a day. This would be almost impossible. By juicing your own fruits and vegetables, it becomes much easier for you to get your daily nutrients without all the bulk. Now, I will say that eating some raw carrots or munching on a crunchy red apple is highly recommended, for you do need your vegetable and fruit fibers (one should not take the place of the other). But juicing can become a great way to introduce water-packed foods into your lifestyle. Think of juicing as providing your supplements and medicines.

To give you an idea of what exactly those fruits and vegetables are going to do for you, I have broken them down by category.

Orange Foods: Orange foods have an excellent effect on reducing pains and cramps. They help strengthen the lungs and support the respiratory system. Emotionally, orange foods help you to feel more joyous and positive. They promote vitality and mental clarity.

Examples: oranges, apricots, pumpkins, carrots, sweet potatoes.

Green Foods: Green leafy vegetables are extremely high in calcium. As a matter of fact, one cup of fresh juiced kale or broccoli is four times more calcium-rich than one cup of milk. Green foods are excellent blood purifiers and bactericides, and create a natural tranquilizing effect.

Examples: kale, broccoli, sprouts, wheat grass, avocados, lettuce

Yellow Foods: Excellent for morning consumption. Yellow foods strengthen your nerves, help in digestion and the relief of constipation, and act as a natural stimulant for early-morning energy.

Examples: lemons, pineapples, grapefruits, peaches, bananas, mangoes, papayas, yellow squash, corn.

Blue Foods: Excellent for headaches, these foods create a sense of calm, centeredness, and focus. They're good when you need to study or concentrate. Blue foods are very cooling to the system and are especially effective on hot summer days.

Examples: blueberries, grapes, plums, potatoes, celery, parsnips, asparagus.

Red Foods: These create heat and circulation. They make excellent juices to consume on cold, blustery days.

Examples: tomatoes, red cabbage, red/hot peppers, cherries, cranberries, radishes.

When first beginning to juice, you may experience a bout of diarrhea, digestive discomfort, and frequent urination. This is because your body is detoxifying and being introduced to high levels of nutrients. It may take some time for you to adjust. I recommend no more than eight ounces of fresh juice three times a day at the beginning of your juicing. Combining fruits and vegetables is a great way to experiment. Have fun and experience the energy.

Now that you have studied the list of foods to fill your system with, I am going to give you a list of foods that create imbalance, causing us to have mood swings, unhealthy thoughts, and lack of physical energy. In JayWalking, the objective is to see the world and experience it at peak performance, being the best we can be. The following is a list of foods that will dull your senses, making you foggy and not able to focus, a far cry from the ultimate fitness journey.

Sugar: Mood swings and unhealthy thoughts are associated with the ingestion of cane and beet sugar, and its counterparts corn syrup, high-fructose corn syrup, and maltodextrin. This sugar is so concentrated that it sends our bodies into a state of shock. It wouldn't be so bad if you were to chew on a stalk of sugarcane. However, one tablespoon of brown or granulated sugar is so concentrated it's like eating a gigantic stalk of sugarcane. Far too much for normal consumption by the human species.

When sugar enters your body, your pancreas secretes large amounts of insulin, a hormone responsible for the breakdown of sugar in the body. With such a high concentration of sugar, our insulin levels skyrocket, giving us the ever-popular sugar high. But as we all know, what goes up must come down, and we soon find ourselves in the dungeon of doom, where we either take a nap or run to our next roller-coaster ride with a candy bar. This vicious circle can continue on and on. Definitely not a good place to achieve healthy thoughts.

White Flour: Papier mâché anyone? Remember mixing white flour with warm water? Dipping newspaper strips into the gooky white mixture? Draping it over a balloon and then waiting for it to harden? Well, gang, that's what you're doing to your system every time you eat white flour in pasta and bread products. The misconception here is that pasta and bread are carbohydrates, and therefore supposedly good for you. The difference, however, is that white flour is a *simple* carbohydrate. It has a high glucidic rate, which means it digests high in sugar—in other words, during the digestive process, your pancreas has to secrete high levels of insulin in order to break down the flour. Constipation is a common side effect from too much white flour. Whole wheat flour is a separate issue. If you try mixing it with warm water, nothing will happen. It won't harden; that's because whole wheat is a *complex* carbohydrate. The glucidic rate is much lower, so your pancreas doesn't have to work so hard, keeping your insulin level balanced, which means less sugar highs and lows and much more fiber.

Turkey: Ever wonder why after Thanksgiving dinner everyone takes a nap? It's that gobble of Tom Turkey. Turkey contains an amino acid called L-tryptophan that promotes sleep, relaxing your brain and slowing down your mental process. Although turkey is one of my favorite foods, and an excellent source of protein for strong, healthy muscles, I wouldn't recommend it to enter the world of Jay-Walking.

Coffee/Caffeine: Much like sugar, coffee will give you that jolt of energy. But beware: Caffeine is a central nervous system stimulant that acts on your adrenal glands, triggering them to release sugar, which is stored in your liver. Your mind will race, and you may experience heart palpitations. Coffee has also a diuretic quality, which can be a nuisance while you are traveling down the road on your Jay-Walking fitness journey.

Aspartame/Saccharin: There has been much controversy about these man-made chemical sweeteners. Aspartame and saccharin have been known to cause severe headaches and cancers, as well as other unhealthy side effects. Much more research needs to be done on these substances. My motto is, if Mother Nature didn't have a hand in it, stay away.

Besides good nutrition, I recommend good living. This means not smoking, limiting your alcohol intake, sleeping at least seven hours a night, working fewer than ten hours a day, exercising and striving for a balanced lifestyle.

THE SPIRITUAL JOURNEY

Our deepest fear is not that we are inadequate. Our deepest fear is that we are powerful beyond measure. It is our light, not our darkness, that frightens us. We ask ourselves, Who am I to be brilliant, gorgeous, talented, and fabulous? Actually, who are you not to be? You are a spiritual being. Your playing small doesn't serve the world. There's nothing enlightened about shrinking so that other people won't feel insecure around you. We are all meant to shine, as children do. We were born to manifest the glory of spirit that is within us. It's not just in some of us; it's in everyone. And as we let our own light shine, we unconsciously give other people permission to do the same. As we are liberated from our own fear, our presence automatically liberates others.

—MARIANNE WILLIAMSON, *A Return to Love*

INTRODUCTION

Unlike the previous two journeys, the Mental and the Physical, the Spiritual Journey is not comprised of techniques and exercises. It is designed to allow you, the reader, to be enlightened by a completely refreshing perception of life's most concerning topics.

The word "spirituality" can be uncomfortable for many individuals. *I would like to stress that when I say "spirit," what I mean is a place within each and every one of you that is kind, joyful, and loving.* This is the superconscious mind, that part of us that receives inspiration and divine ideas. The superconsciousness is free from punishment. It is pure, innocent, loving, and faithful.

In the Spiritual Journey, you will have amazing revelations concerning how we judge life, the world, and the people we come in contact with. Each section ends with an antidote, to help your JayWalking journey enhance your perception in a healthy way. I have added affirmations that can be applied to your JayWalking journey at any point throughout the day. This section will assist you in creating more value as an individual, and align with your higher self. This section springs from the philosophy that if your spirit puts you on hold, do not hang up.

SPIRIT

Like a sheet of music, spirit must be played
to experience its wonder.

—OLGA BUTTERWORTH

The spirit is astonishing. It is the only part of our being that lives eternally. The spirit is the only part of us that can recognize the truth (that love is the healing force). It is, however, very unfortunate that in this society we have become so detached from the spirit, the truth, the part of ourselves that holds all of the answers to life on earth.

We have all experienced some degree of starvation of spirit. If we take a look around us, we see how the world needs that connection to spirit: *the wars, bloodshed, famine, verbal and emotional abuse, lack of intimacy, lack of communication, abandonment—all stemming from the need for spirituality.* The spirit is secure; it knows itself; it connects with all of the energy around it. It cannot be unexpressed; for if the spirit is contained and not expressed, the physical body and emotional intellect will begin to break down, in turn creating imbalance, turmoil, and disease. With the connection of spirit in our lives, we begin to express ourselves indefinitely, with a nonaggressive strength, in kinship and wholeness, infinitely, on this wonderful planet Earth.

LOVE

And love can come to everyone,

for the best things in life are free.

—BUDDY DE SYLVA

Songs are constantly written about it, and we humans will search to the ends of the earth to experience its hidden mysteries. What is it about love that makes us feel so good? Is it the intimacy, the security, or the pleasure, that keeps us coming back for more? Or do the answers lie much deeper, beyond our external experiences?

A team of doctors and scientists conducted a study on individuals who had all experienced death for a short period of time. All of their stories were uncannily similar. They all saw a vision of bright light and had a sense of peace and tranquility during the experience. However, the highlight was that they all saw their lives flash in front of them, from birth up to the near-death experience—and the most painful parts of their life movie were times when they hadn't expressed their love.

Love is a force, as real as gravity. It is the spirit in its purest form. Love was intended by the universe to be our natural state. As infants, we enter the world completely loved and lovable. We are, in essence, the truest expression of love. But as time goes by, experiences in life, like betrayal, abandonment, and anger, to name but a few, do a lot to obliterate our feelings of love. It is at this point that we begin to experience the separation from spirit. We begin to think that love is outside of us. After all, it shows up in all of those external experiences—attractive people, fast cars, expensive clothes, exotic vacations—and seeing is believing, or so we've been told.

This is when the tug-of-war begins, between the internal and the external. Because we see love as something outside ourselves we must somehow "get," we begin to choose fear over love, and by choosing fear, we produce pain. Fear is ego-based. It is the opposite of love. By choosing love, we are producing pleasure—and pleasure is a healing force.

JayWalking will take you away from fear. The moment-to-moment experiences of being in the here and now will make you give way to joy. By experiencing joy, you will see that it's not what a person does that counts, it's the gift in their doing. For example: Let's say someone donates money to charity simply to look good. Even though this person's intention is not coming from a place of purity, the act of giving is still benefiting the needy (it's all in what we choose to see). As we become more loving, our spirits will begin to reveal more and more gifts that we never would have perceived before.

Don't look for lack; look for the love within you and all of mankind. When, and only when, you trust that love is at the core of your nature, will you begin to not simply feel love, but be love. The

following affirmation is meant to remind you of the importance of
love during those fearful times

> SPIRIT, REVEAL TO ME ALL OF THE LOVE THAT SURROUNDS ME.
>
> HELP ME SURRENDER ALL OF MY JUDGMENTS OF MANKIND,
>
> THAT I MAY SEE PERFECTION IN ALL HUMANITY.
>
> SHOW ME HOW TO LOVE, AND TO BE LOVED.

SELF

Very little is needed to make a happy life.

—MARCUS AURELIUS

Solitary time, the time in which we JayWalk, is our passageway
to spirituality. It is a time when we release any doubts or questions
we may have on what our purpose in life is. Many of us feel we don't
know our purpose in this world. This is because we haven't spent
enough quiet time alone with spirit. Why haven't we? Because when
we're alone, we begin to get bored or restless. We will do anything to
keep ourselves moving—chatting on the telephone, switching on the
TV, running down to a favorite store for a box of Devil Dogs, or just
napping for lack of something better to do. We pay an extremely high
price for being so conditioned to "get busy" as quickly as possible.
Because we don't connect with spirit, we experience feelings of violation, dysfunction, sickness, addiction, limitation, and weakness. All
of these feelings bring us further away from our sense of self, creating havoc and leaving our spirit in turmoil.

JayWalking requires practice—practice in being in the present
moment and unleashing your spirit's true nature. You may become
too concerned that you're not JayWalking properly, but you need to
remember that this is just your mind creating resistance with the tornado of thoughts. This chaos allows us to be pulled further away
from the moment. When you JayWalk on a regular basis, your spirit
will begin to reveal itself. You will begin to experience a self that is
not weak but strong, a self that has unlimited capabilities, a self in

peace: loving, serene, calm, and happy—all from the connection of spirit.

SPIRIT, SHOW ME HOW TO LOVE MYSELF.

TEACH ME TO STAY FOCUSED ON MY INNER GIFTS,

SO THAT I CAN EXPRESS THEM AND SHARE

MY WONDER WITH THE WORLD.

RELATIONSHIPS

Relationships are like a book, in that they are for learning.

—MARSHALL SYLVER

Relationships bring us to a place of balance in our lives. If we look around us, we will find that relationships extend beyond human form. The relationships we have with the trees, the flowers, the sunshine, and the seasons all bring us to a state of balance. This is why we seek so innately for a partner in our lives when what we're looking for is that connection to spirit, for relationships are part of our spirit. The belief is that by bringing another into our life, we will create a place of balance or harmony. But too many times we find ourselves connecting mostly with the superficial aspects of another person—their charm, their title, their money, and their looks—realizing only later on that these are all masks that cover the true self. It is their spirit that we are initially attracted to. In every relationship we teach either love or fear. If we express love, we learn how to love more deeply. If we demonstrate fear or negativity, we learn to denounce or finger-point, and become more frightened of life.

When we JayWalk, we begin to experience a relationship not only with nature, but with the true essence of ourselves. The Jay-Walking fitness journey will bring forth all of your talents, enabling you to love yourself that much more. When you truly love yourself, you will not be persuaded by the external looks of another individual. This has no relation to the person's natural appearance. In other words, by JayWalking, you will come in contact with your true self, your breathing, your emotions, and the way you look at nature, not just in a broad spectrum, but in complete and vivid detail, down to the little dewdrops cascading off of a colorful autumn leaf. You will have a higher appreciation for what you see, so that the relationships you have will become more than what meets the eye. You will also have a higher appreciation for people— what they're about and where they're coming from. By treating people with compassion, forgiveness, and love, you are more likely to activate a healing response. People will be less likely to be defensive and will be more open to learning. In essence, you'll be harmonizing with their subliminal rhythms. Rhythm is a great communicator, and if we're self-involved, each in our own rhythm, we won't be taking the time to slow down and investigate other people for who they truly are. By traveling down the JayWalking road to fitness, you will become more in tune to the natural rhythms of other individuals and be able to find relationships from deep within.

SPIRIT, HELP ME HEAL MY RESISTANCE TO LOVE.

SHOW ME ALL OF THE BEAUTY THAT SURROUNDS ME,

SO THAT I MAY FIND IT IN THE SIMPLEST OF RELATIONSHIPS.

MAY I BECOME A MAGNET OF YOUR LOVE, AND A SHIELD FOR FEAR.

ANGER/HOSTILITY

The most useless day of all is that
in which we have not laughed.

—SEBASTIEN ROCH NICOLAS CHAMFORT

In a small seaport town off the southern coast of Italy lies a rare species of jellyfish. This jellyfish travels the seafloor to gobble up anything in its path. It has a very curious interest for a specific type of snail. When the jellyfish consumes the snail, an amazing and remarkable reaction takes place. The snail then attaches itself to the inner wall of the jellyfish. As time goes by, the snail begins to eat its way through until it has completely consumed the jellyfish and all that remains is a happy, hearty, smiling snail.

If we pause for a moment to think about our lives, and look at the angers and hostilities that have gone unexpressed or have been expressed in unhealthy ways, we can see how our lives are on a parallel course to the jellyfish. We absorb these unhealthy emotions and feelings and don't know how to express them or digest them, until they begin to eat at us and manifest themselves in either disease, sickness, hatred, or hostility. Without the proper awareness of these hidden angers, we begin a spiraling descent into unhappiness, misery, and discontent. How, then, do we find peace and release any hidden angers and hatreds we might have? Think for a moment of your past. Is there an unpleasant situation that may have transpired between you and a schoolmate that you have never released? Or maybe a hostile word from your mother that you took personally? All of these thoughts and emotions are being stored in your subconscious mind. Unless they are freed in a healthy way, you will continue to experience adversities throughout life.

Energy is a valuable commodity. Each and every day we are given a certain amount. Some days more, some days less. If our past angers and hatreds are not addressed and freed, we are using this valuable energy in an unconstructive way.

When you JayWalk, you are given the ability to free your emotional state through an increase in oxygen uptake. Focusing on your breathing or the beauty in the surrounding environment will soften your thought process and your emotions. This is a wonderful way of communicating with your spirit. The quiet silent time will begin to release any anger or hostility that you may have. The great thing about JayWalking is that you can use the anger and hostility in a constructive way. By JayWalking and working out your body the anger becomes fuel and energy for the physical workout. The anger is then used for something positive in the development of your physical body, as opposed to something negative, such as hostile thoughts and feelings toward others, overeating, excessive alcohol consumption, cigarette smoking, or any other physically destructive activity.

SPIRIT, ASSIST ME IN RELEASING MY RESENTMENTS
TOWARD OTHER PEOPLE AND EVENTS.
REVEAL TO ME HEALTHY WAYS TO EXPRESS MY ANGER SO I
MAY BE EMPOWERED AND ABLE TO GIVE LOVE.

PROSPERITY

Lack nothing: be merry.

—SHAKESPEARE

As you sit and read this book, you are benefiting from the prosperity that surrounds you. Sunlight, fresh air, the clean water you drink and bathe in, the whispering winds to cool your body, paved highways to travel down, and a variety of foods to please your palate—all are at your disposal. For a moment, just relish that thought. When you feel lack in your life, remind yourself of where you live, of how much prosperity is available to you, and how blessed you are to be a part of it. Not feeling prosperous in our lives stems from how we're focusing. If I focus on lack of material things, that's exactly what I will receive on an emotional level: lack, emptiness, and no fulfillment, regardless of my actual material prosperity.

I remember one morning awakening within anger. I was frustrated because I had not been living the lifestyle I had once envisioned for myself. The bigger home, bright red sports car, and designer clothes—all of these material things that I had thought would give me peace of mind seemed out of reach. And the more I focused on them, the more depressed I got. What my spirit was craving was an inner peace, a silence, that the pressures of society could not take away. I got dressed and went for my morning JayWalk. I remember vividly focusing on my breathing, watching its natural rhythm, like the ticking of a metronome. I felt very meditative that morning. And then the answer I was looking for hit me. It wasn't the security of material wealth I was seeking, it was the fulfillment of serenity instead. I began to take note of all of the riches that already existed in my life (my health, my dog, the roof over my head, my friends, my mind, my spirit, the gift of choice). How much more prosperity could I expect when I didn't even acknowledge what I had.

When I JayWalk I go to that quiet place within. It is in the stillness that all answers are revealed to me. In the simpleness of *not doing,* the part of us that doesn't feed into the tornado of thoughts, one finds prosperity in the calm of the moment.

It may seem easy to find comfort when you have material wealth, but to be comfortable within when you don't is to be in touch with spirit.

SPIRIT, RELEASE ME FROM MY ANXIETIES ABOUT MATERIAL
WEALTH. REVEAL TO ME ALL OF MY INTERNAL ABUNDANCE,
SO THAT I MAY BE A GIVER OF YOUR TALENTS
(INTERNAL ABUNDANCE PRODUCES EXTERNAL ABUNDANCE).

CAREER/WORK

Only lifelong work entitles a man to say:
I have lived.

—GOETHE

The more we work, the more we produce. The more we work, the more money we make. The more we work, the better our work will be. These beliefs place us on a treadmill of anxiety, frustration, and aggression. We become so caught up in the actual production of work that we lose touch with the benefits it brings to our day, not on a physical level, as in money or authority, but on a spiritual level. It's amazing to think that in the present day the average worker is working 138 hours more in one year than his or her counterpart did 20 years earlier. It is true that we are gaining more goods—the cars, the homes, the clothes, the vacations, not to mention the bills—but at what expense have these material things been acquired if we are negating our health and creating anxiety?

Susan, a client of mine, once revealed to me how anxious she was to go back to singing lessons. I turned to her and asked if she could find time after work for her lessons. "I don't know," she responded, "my job is so unpredictable, I couldn't schedule anything else into my day. I'm afraid if I don't keep working, I'll lose my job or turn out like people who never get anything accomplished in life." At that moment it dawned on me that Susan was suffering from a case of low self-esteem, and that the fear of expressing her singing talents was keeping her trapped in her job.

The real issue here is our reluctance to face the emotional discomfort we feel with our jobs and our careers. It would take a lot of practice and a lot of uncomfortable feelings for us to sit quietly and relax and reveal to ourselves what we are truly feeling about our jobs. We have become so conditioned to the habitual speedy rhythm of work that it seems easier to keep doing it rather than to feel the discomfort that might come up if we were to slow down. But if we don't learn to slow down and shift our gears, the stress will eventually get us—in one way or another.

By participating in the JayWalking fitness program, you will experience a sense of accomplishment. You can bring about this sense of accomplishment just by showing up, for you are interrupting the normal daily pattern and introducing a brand-new program. By instilling a pattern of accomplishment into our day, we can feel better about our tasks at work, and this will help release our fears of not achieving in the workplace. You'll become more aware of how your body feels when you JayWalk, how all of your built-in talents are revealed, and your new connection to spirit. By noticing these simple gifts, you can begin to release the pressures of work, and this awareness will give you a higher appreciation for what work *is*. Work is *not* about "making a living." Work is not about "putting in time." Work is about being in the here and now. Try it!

SPIRIT, SHOW ME HOW TO RELEASE ANY STRUGGLES I
MAY HAVE WITH MY CAREER/WORK.
TEACH ME TO BE A VEHICLE FOR CREATIVITY, PASSION,
AND BRILLIANCE, SO MY WORK
WILL EXPRESS MY UNIQUE GIFTS.

TIME

In truth, paradise is where you are right now.

—STEPHAN RECHTSCHAFFEN

Six-thirty A.M., Thursday, New York Sports Club. The scheduled time of the JayWalking Fitness Journey, and the winding down of my busy workweek.

I arrive at the club at 6:30 on the dot, and I am greeted by the scowling presence of irate and agitated members. "Let's go! It's already 6:31!" "I'm going to be late for work!" "You're always late, Jay!" "Is everything all right?" One frustrated woman tells me that I have a problem, that I'm always running late, and I need to get some help.

And good morning to you too! Not to give you the wrong impression of my students; I love them all dearly. The education I share with them I get back twofold. So how come we become so stressed about time? It seems as though we wear time around our ankles, like a ball and chain, becoming slaves to the clock. Now, I'm not saying that clock time shouldn't be valued. After all, it is the Western way of living and sometimes that gives us order. But by not slowing down, we will constantly be left with something missing—an emptiness, a void.

Looking at our watches, and knowing what time it is, gives us the impression of stability and security. But this is only a one-dimensional view of time, and by perceiving time in this fashion, we're neglecting our spirit.

We seem to place everything but ourselves and our spirit first. Work, routine chores, relationships, family life, social responsibilities—all take precedence over ourselves and our spirit. We begin to feel frustrated, stressed, pressured, and anxious. All because we look at time in only one dimension—not having enough.

In colonial times, land, crops, clothes, and food all had to be harvested or prepared by hand. This took countless hours to complete. And the individuals performing these tasks had none of our modern-day timesaving devices: cell phones, electricity, e-mail, speed dialing, fax machines, computers (all of which add speed— and stress—to our lives.) So how can we explain that these individuals had such a zest for life, unlike us modern-day people? Wedding ceremonies lasted for more than five days; celebrations of seasons, harvests, and holidays would last for a week. There was more joy, friendliness, and love.

In JayWalking, we lose track of time. For we are really learning how to experience being in the here and now. Our external focus on trees, colors, shapes, and sounds, and our internal focus on affirmations, breathing, positive visualizations, and nonjudgment of emotions, bring us to a place of tranquility. So instead of seeing time as wasted, we seem to find new time. When we change our perception of the moment, we lose track of time, and it begins to surround us and not run past us. In essence, we become one with it.

> SPIRIT, SHOW ME HOW TO RELAX. HELP ME BECOME AWARE
> THAT TIME IS INFINITE. REVEAL TO ME THE BEAUTY THAT IS
> ALWAYS PRESENT. BRING ME TO A CALM AND LOVING PLACE.
> I AM RIGHT WHERE I NEED TO BE.

DEATH

The fear of death is more to be dreaded than death itself.

—PUBLILIUS SYRUS

When we're alive, death seems far in the future. If we begin to worry about death, we essentially begin living in the future. By bringing the future into the present, we create a future of thought, just like the past. By letting our thoughts of death go, we make room for miracles. Remember: *The thoughts of death rob us of life in the present.* It is much better to remain in the here and now, where the wonder and joy exist.

Death is a continuum. One never really dies in physical form. It is true there is a loss. But with the realization of spirit, and the knowing that the true essence of a person is not the body and not the external things that the person represents, we can gently release the hold the loss of the body has on us.

My belief is that if a person's spirit has touched your spirit, it will never leave your side. The human form may not be with you, but the spiritual gifts you have received were given to you forever. Many of us seem to allow our fears to interfere with gifts of joy. We look at death as a loss, not trusting spirit to guide us to an inner peace in the matter. Death is both the end and the beginning. We are all in the process of evolution. We don't know when it will happen, so why not express our love and our issues now, before it's too late?

One way to get in touch with your feelings about death is through JayWalking. For when you JayWalk, you are experiencing a beginning and an end, which is very similar to the cycle of life and death. By becoming conditioned to being in the here and now, we build a sense of security and confidence within ourselves that enables us to control our feelings more appropriately in times of turmoil. We can begin to become more comfortable with the concept of death.

SPIRIT, RELEASE ME FROM MY PAINFUL AND LIMITED BELIEFS. GUIDE ME TO A PLACE OF KNOWLEDGE, SO THAT I MAY OPEN MY EYES FROM THE ILLUSION OF DEATH AND SEE THE WONDER OF ETERNAL LIFE.

AGING

No man loves life like him that's growing old.

—SOPHOCLES

The cosmetics industry is a multibillion-dollar industry, one of the most profit-generating industries in our country. It is amazing that we Americans will strive at any cost to eliminate the most minuscule wrinkle, for fear it will spread into a road map of destruction. Aging is a depressing thought. It reminds us that we're never as we were in the past. It takes us farther and farther away from what seem to be our moments of true power. It reminds us that we're *on our way out.*

Our Western belief is that our scientific advancements and technology will supply us with all the answers. We start to think that information is more valid than wisdom and experience, so that as we age, we become useless understudies or even a burden to society.

This is a very sad belief system, one I have always searched to find answers to. I always wondered why some of my clients in their seventies and eighties appeared to be slow-moving, depressive, and glum, while others are vivacious, radiant, and full of life. Ria, a client of mine in her late seventies, began walking with me more than two years ago. Her fitness level was very poor, and she had a slight limp. However, I was amazed by her bubbly attitude. She wasn't concerned whether or not she would be at the front of the group or able to keep up with the exercises; her interest was more in getting to know each of my clients individually and fully experiencing the beauty that surrounded her, and how the outdoor activity made her feel. She was a true student, a constant learner, who participated in the here and now. This kept her spirit active. It kept her growing, and you could see the spirit radiating in her expressions.

Aging is a learned behavior. Selective groups of doctors and scientists believe that aging is brought on not by our biological clocks but by what we have heard and learned over and over again. Unlike plants, trees, and animals, humans have a higher intelligence. We have the power of choice. So why choose to live with a belief that as we get old time passes quickly, and that there's nothing new for us to learn because we've been through it all, and that our bodies aren't functioning as they did in the past? Why not adopt a new belief? That aging is an opportunity for us to expand our moments so that we are more present in the now. The more practice we have being in the present today, the better we'll be able to cope with aging tomorrow.

Harvard University conducted a study in 1979 to see if our thoughts affected our aging. Two groups of people 75 and over were recruited for a one-week vacation with all expenses paid to a fabulous country estate. Group A was brought to an environment where all was recreated like the 1950s: the radio played music of that era, there were newspapers, Academy Award–winning films shown, and a speech by President Eisenhower. Group A was encouraged to focus on how they looked, talked, and behaved more than 20 years earlier. They were asked to speak of the events of the 1950s in the present tense. Group B was brought to an environment of the 1970s, and was encouraged to talk about the 1950s only in the past tense. The radio played music of the present time, and individuals talked about current affairs.

The results were astonishing. After one week, Group A became more physically active. They were more responsible for their tasks, their fingers became more flexible, and the length of their fingers even grew. Vision and hearing improved. Group B, on the other hand, showed few, if any, signs of improvement. It is clear that the power of positive thinking can make us forever youthful.

JayWalking can take us to a place where we're truly present. It doesn't matter if the here and now is momentous or ordinary, for there isn't any judgment. What matters is this: When you're in the JayWalking moment, you won't just be doing something in order to get it done, you won't simply be going through the motions of life. It is the aging attitude that makes the days, the months, and the years begin to recede and makes us no longer have the appreciation for life. By JayWalking in the moment, you will recapture the youthfulness of spirit.

SPIRIT, UNFOLD THE WONDER AND EXCITEMENT IN EVERY
MOMENT OF MY LIFE.
HELP ME TO SEE THE POWER I HAVE BEEN GIVEN TO CHANGE
ALL PERCEPTION AROUND ME.
REVIVE AND RENEW MY YOUTHFUL SPONTANEITY.

HEALTH

You should pray for a sound mind in a sound body.

—JUVENAL

Ideal health is a by-product of spirit. If we can establish a habit in consciousness that we *are* spirit, we can have the power to enjoy optimum health.

The body is not a lump of flesh. It is a mass of independent, intelligent cells. These cells are capable of being directed, just as we direct our arms and legs to move when we JayWalk. If we tap into the intelligent center of our spirit, being in the here and now, we will reestablish health and harmony.

Illness develops when we see ourselves as body and not as spirit. The body is a mirror of inner thoughts and beliefs. What you see is what you get. Illness is the spirit in disguise. The problem with illness is that it tempts us to focus on the body when we need mainly to focus on the spirit. In order to heal the body, we must believe that it is not who we are. For our spirit is eternally healthy. The spirit's function is to experience, express, and communicate love, which transcends the body.

Support groups for true healing are designed not so one can grow closer to his or her disease, but so that people can build a closer relationship with their spirit. This is where the healing lies. Individuals in healing groups should be encouraged to become still, focus on their breathing, and internally have a conversation with their illness. They should be encouraged to find out what it is saying. This is the first step toward acknowledging the spirit. Stillness reveals many messages. When we are still, we can begin to see where all our judgments lie.

Man is a creature of habit, and most difficulties of life are a result of bad habits. Limited thinking can become a habit as well. By accepting yourself as whole in spirit, you can begin to erase the habits of limitation and to form habits of joy.

JayWalking will release you from bad habits by instilling a new habit, a habit of being in the here and now, and increasing your tolerance for physical difficulty by developing physical strength.

Strength comes from being relaxed, powerful, and peaceful. Unhappiness is designed to *un*happen things. Let them happen and work on the habit of health.

SPIRIT, YOU ARE WHOLE, PURE, AND COMPLETE. HELP ME TO BE STILL, AND TO FIND FOR MYSELF THAT MY HEALTH IS FOREVER WHOLE.

RELEASE ME FROM JUDGMENT, FEAR, AND PAIN.

Congratulations, you have done it, and I am proud of you. You have completed *JayWalking: The Ultimate Fitness Journey*. The rest is up to you. I wish you the best of luck and my love on your future journeys.

BIBLIOGRAPHY

Without the material from these spectacular authors this book could not have been written. I thank each and every one and suggest that you experience their talents individually.

Reading is to the mind what exercise is to the body.

—SIR RICHARD STEELE

Bandler, Richard. *Using Your Brain for a Change.* 1985.

———. *Refraining.* Distributers TH, 1988.

Bartlett, John. *Familiar Quotations.* Emily Morison Beck (ed.). 14th edition. Boston: Little, Brown and Company, 1968.

———. *A Complete Concordance or Verbal Index to Words, Phrases and Passages in the Dramatic Works of Shakespeare With a Supplementary Concordance to the Poems.* London: Macmillan & Co Ltd, 1960.

Benson, Herbert, and Eileen M. Stuart. *The Wellness Book.* New York: Fireside, 1992.

Benson, Herbert, with Marg Stark. *Timeless Healing*. New York: Scribner, 1996.

Berry, Carmen Renee. *Your Body Never Lies*. Berkeley, Calif.: PageMill Press, 1993.

The Book of Massage. New York: Simon & Schuster, 1984.

Breathnach, Sarah Ban. *Simple Abundance*. New York: Warner Books, Inc., 1995.

Buscaglia, Leo F. *Loving Each Other*. New York: Fawcett Columbine, 1984.

Butler, Gillian, and Tony Hope. *Managing Your Mind*. New York: Oxford University Press, Inc., 1995.

Canfield, Jack, and Mark Victor Hansen. *Chicken Soup for the Soul*. Deerfield Beach, Florida: Health Communications, Inc., 1993.

―――. *The Aladdin Factor*. New York: Berkley Books, 1995.

Carper, Jean. *Stop Aging Now!* New York: HarperCollins Publishers, Inc., 1995.

Chopra, Deepak. *Ageless Body, Timeless Mind*. New York: Harmony Books, 1993.

―――. *The Seven Spiritual Laws of Success*. San Rafael, Calif.: Amber-Allen Publishing and New World Library, 1994.

―――. *The Path to Love*. New York: Random House, 1997.

Cotton, Richard T. (managing ed.), Robert L. Goldstein (ed.). *Aerobics Instructor Manual*. San Diego, Calif.: American Council on Exercise; Boston: Reebok University Press, 1993.

Day, Laura. *Practical Intuition*. New York: Villard Books, 1996.

Doré, Carole. *Visualization Through the Heart*. Newport Beach, Calif.: PowerVision Dynamics, 1986.

Dufty, William. *Sugar Blues*. New York: Warner Books, Inc., 1975.

Friedman, Philip, and Gail Eisen. *The Pilates Method of Physical and Mental Conditioning.* New York: Warner Books, Inc., 1981.

Gach, Michael Reed. *Acupressure's Potent Points.* New York: Bantam Books, 1990.

Gawain, Shakti. *Creative Visualization.* Novato, Calif.: New World Library, 1995.

Goethe, Johann Wolfgang von. *Goethe's World View.* Frederick Ungar (ed.). New York: Frederick Ungar Publishing Co., 1963.

Gray, Henry. *Gray's Anatomy.* 15th edition. T. Pickering Pick, Robert Howden (eds.). New York: Barnes & Noble Books, 1995.

Hay, Louise L. *You Can Heal Your Life.* Carlsbad, Calif.: Hay House, Inc., 1984.

Hillman, Carolynn. *Love Your Looks.* New York: Fireside, 1996.

Jeffers, Susan. *Feel the Fear and Do It Anyway.* New York: Fawcett Columbine, 1987.

———. *End the Struggle and Dance With Life.* New York: St. Martin's Press, 1996.

Jolley, Willie. *It Only Takes a Minute to Change Your Life!* New York: St. Martin's Paperbacks, 1997.

Kabat-Zinn, Jon. *Wherever You Go There You Are.* New York: Hyperion, 1994.

Katselas, Milton. *Dreams Into Action.* Beverly Hills, Calif.: Dove Books, 1996.

Lad, Vasant. *Ayurveda: The Science of Self-Healing.* Wilmot, Wisc.: Lotus Light, 1994.

Lavin, Edward J., S. J. *Life Meditations.* New York: Wings Books, 1993.

Levine, Suzanne. *Walk It Off!* New York: Plume, 1990.

McMahon, Susanna. *The Portable Therapist*. New York: Dell Publishing, 1992.

McWilliams, Peter. *The Portable Do It!* Los Angeles: Prelude Press, 1995.

Mascaró, Juan (translator). *The Dhammapada*. London: Penguin Books, 1973.

Matthews, Andrew. *Being Happy!* Los Angeles: Price Stern Sloan, Inc., 1988.

Meyerowitz, Steven. *Juice Fasting*. Great Barrington, Mass.: The Sprout House, 1984.

Meyers, Casey. *Walking: A Complete Guide to the Complete Exercise*. New York: Random House, 1992.

Moore, Thomas. *Care of the Soul*. New York: HarperPerennial, 1992.

Moyers, Bill. *Healing and the Mind*. Betty Sue Flowers (ed.), David Grubin (executive editor). New York: Doubleday, 1993.

Nioche, Brigitte. *Dress to Impress*. London: Janus Publishing Company, 1994.

Peck, Scott. *The Road Less Traveled*. New York: Simon & Schuster, 1978.

Rahula, Walpola. *What the Buddha Taught*. New York: Grove Weidenfeld, 1959.

Rechtschaffen, Stephan. *Time Shifting*. New York: Doubleday, 1996.

Redfield, James. *The Celestine Prophecy*. New York: Warner Books, Inc., 1993.

Rives, David A. *Walk Yourself Thin*. Ventura, Calif.: Moon River Publishing, 1994.

Robbins, Anthony. *Notes from a Friend*. New York: Fireside, 1991.

———. *Awaken the Giant Within*. New York: Simon & Schuster, 1992.

———. *Personal Power II: The Driving Force*. San Diego, Calif.: Robbins Research International, 1993.

———. *Unlimited Power*. New York: Ballantine Books, 1996.

Roberts, Keli. *Fitness Hollywood*. Fort Worth, Texas: The Summit Group, 1995.

Sarno, John E. *Healing Back Pain*. New York: Warner Books, Inc., 1991.

Shin, Florence Scovel. *The Game of Life and How to Play It*. Marina del Rey, Calif.: DeVorss & Company, 1925.

Smith, Kathy, with Susanna Levin. *Kathy Smith's Walkfit™ for a Better Body*. New York: Warner Books, Inc., 1994.

Somer, Elizabeth. *Food & Mood*. New York: Henry Holt, 1995.

Spillane, Mary, and Christine Sherlock. *Color Me Beautiful's Looking Your Best: Color, Makeup, and Style*. Lanham, Md.: Madison Books, 1995.

Sudy, Mitchell (ed.). *Personal Trainer Manual*. San Diego, Calif.: American Council on Exercise; Boston: Reebok University Press, 1991.

Stedman's Medical Dictionary. 26th edition. Baltimore: The Williams & Wilkins Company, 1995.

Trudeau, Kevin. *Kevin Trudeau's Mega™ Memory*. New York: William Morrow and Company, Inc., 1995.

Vickery, Donald M., and James F. Fries.*Taking Care of Yourself*. New York: Addison-Wesley Publishing Company, Inc., 1990.

Walking Fit. Emmaus, Pa.: Rodale Press, Inc., 1997.

Webster's Third New International Dictionary. Philip Babcock Gove (ed.-in-chief). Springfield, Mass.: Merriam-Webster, 1986.

Williamson, Marianne. *A Return to Love*. New York: HarperPerennial, 1992.

———. *Illuminata*. New York: Riverhead Books, 1994.

ABOUT THE AUTHOR

Jay Ciniglio, also known as the JayWalker, is an American Council on Exercise–certified fitness motivator and creator, and president of the most successful and dynamic walking program in New York City. He also consults as the walking coach for the New York chapter of the Leukemia Society of America and has been featured in several national publications including *GQ*, *Self*, *Fitness*, *Shape*, *New Woman*, and *Exercise for Men*. Jay has been seen on national television and has traveled the world spreading the Zen-like philosophy that fitness cannot be measured on a scale but is an attitude and must be experienced in the moment. Jay continues his quest to assist individuals to fitness freedom and express their natural gifts, inner beauty and health. Jay resides in New York City with his fitness dog, Misha.

For more information on the JayWalking fitness program or lectures, bimonthly newsletter "The JayWalker," or to become a member of our "On the Road" travel hikes, please write to:

> JayWalking
> P.O. Box 6653
> New York, New York 10128

Take responsibility: become a JayWalker.